Indian Myths of South Central California

By

Alfred Louis Kroeber

First published in 1907

Published by Left of Brain Books

ISBN 978-1-396-32574-8

First Edition

PUBLISHER'S PREFACE

About the Book

"This covers the mythology of the Costanoans, today known as the Ohlone, who lived in the San Francisco and Monterey Bay area; and the Yokuts, who lived in the San Joaquin Valley."

(Quote from sacred-texts.com)

About the Author

Alfred Louis Kroeber (1876 - 1960)

"Alfred Louis Kroeber (June 11, 1876-October 5, 1960) was one of the most influential figures in American anthropology in the first half of the twentieth century.

Kroeber was born in Hoboken, New Jersey. He received his doctorate under Franz Boas at Columbia University in 1901, basing his dissertation on his field work among the Arapaho. He spent most of his career in California, primarily at the University of California, Berkeley where he worked as both a Professor of Anthropology and the Director of what was then The University of California Museum of Anthropology (now the Phoebe A. Hearst Museum of Anthropology). The anthropology department's headquarters building at the University of California is known as Kroeber Hall.

Although he is known primarily as a cultural anthropologist, he did significant work in archaeology, and he contributed to anthropology by making connections between archaeology and culture. He conducted excavations in New Mexico, Mexico, and Peru. Kroeber and his students did important work collecting cultural data on western tribes of Native Americans. The work done in preserving California tribes appeared in Handbook of Indians of California (1925). These efforts to preserve remaining data on these tribes has been termed "Salvage ethnography." He is credited with developing the concepts of Culture Area and Culture Configuration (Cultural and Natural Areas of Native North America, 1939).

His influence was so strong that many contemporaries adopted his style of beard and mustache as well as his views as a social scientist. During his lifetime, he was known as the "Dean of American anthropologists". His anthropological paradigms have introduced the word Kroeberian into the English language. Kroeber and Roland Dixon were very influential in the genetic classification of Native American languages in North America, being responsible for groupings such as Penutian and Hokan. He is noted for working with Ishi, who was claimed (though not uncontroversially) to be the last California Yahi Indian. His second wife, Theodora Kroeber, wrote a well-known biography of Ishi, Ishi in Two Worlds. Kroeber's relationship with Ishi was made into a film The Last of His Tribe (1992), starring Jon Voigt as Kroeber. His textbook, Anthropology (1923, 1948), was widely used for years.

Kroeber was father of the academic Karl Kroeber and the fantasy writer Ursula K. Le Guin by his second wife, Theodora. He also adopted the two children of Theodora's first marriage, Ted and historian Clifton Kroeber. Clifton and Karl recently (2003) edited a book together on the Ishi case, Ishi in Three Centuries. This is the first scholarly book on Ishi to contain essays by Indians."

(Quote from wikipedia.org)

CONTENTS

INTRODUCTION

THE material on which this paper is based was collected in the years 1901 to 1906 as part of the work of the Ethnological and Archaeological Survey of California carried on by the University of California's Department of Anthropology, which owes its existence and continued support to the interest of Mrs. Phoebe A. Hearst.

California presents three principal ethnological divisions. First, in the extreme northwest of the state, bordering on the Pacific Ocean and Oregon, is a small area whose native culture is fundamentally isolated to an unusual degree. Second, in the region commonly known as Southern California, that is to say the territory south of Tehachapi pass in the interior and of Point Concepcion on the coast, there is some diversity of ethnological conditions, but the area as a whole is quite distinctly marked off from the remainder of the state. Third, there is the remaining two-thirds of the state, an area which has been called, in an ethnological sense, and in distinction from the Northwestern and Southern areas, the Central region. This central region consists of what is ordinarily known as northern California and central California, two areas of about equal extent lying north and south of the latitude of San Francisco. Northern California is constituted by the Sacramento valley and the adjacent portions of the Sierra Nevada and Coast Range; central California, by the San Joaquin valley and the parts of the same mountain ranges contiguous to it. The Sacramento valley drains southward, the San Joaquin valley northward. The drainage of both enters the ocean at San Francisco; so that the selection of this city to mark the separation of the northern odd southern halves of the Central region is not fortuitous.

The of northwestern California is still rather imperfectly represented by collections of traditions, but its general characteristics have been discussed in a paper on "Wishosk Myths" in a recent number of the Journal of American Folklore.[1] The mythology of the Central region, both northern and southern, is treated in the present paper. That of the northern half is comparatively well known through several collections, and will be summarized here. That of the southern half,--south central California,--is very little known, but is illustrated by the new material which constitutes the present paper. The mythology of Southern California is quite distinct from that of the Northwestern and Central regions, and deserves separate discussion.[2]

MYTHOLOGY OF THE NORTHERN CENTRAL REGION

There are two principal published collections of myths from the Indians of the northern half of the Central region: Dixon's "Maidu Myths"[3] and Curtin's "Creation Myths of Primitive America."[4] These two works illustrate the mythology of three linguistic families, the Maidu, Wintun, and Yana. Smaller publications, together with the various material available to the author as a result of the work of the Ethnological and Archaeological Survey of California, serve to give some idea of the traditions of this whole northern Central region. The most general characteristics of this mythology include a marked development of true creation ideas, with the participation of Coyote in a role more or less opposed to that of the Creator; the absence of migration or historical traditions; the importance of hero and destroyer myths, and the general prevalence of animal characters. These characteristics as compared with the mythological traits of Northwestern California have been set forth in the before-mentioned paper on Wishosk Myths. It remains now to examine and summarize this north Central material in order to compare it more fully with the material which was obtained and is here newly presented from the south Central region.

Maidu

With a few exceptions, the Maidu myths given by Dr. Dixon were collected at two points, Genesee in Plumas county and Chico in Butte county. They are representative therefore of two of the three principal divisions of the Maidu, the northeastern and the northwestern. In the northwestern division Dr. Dixon distinguishes between the inhabitants of the Sacramento valley and those of the foothill region. Chico being situated on the Sacramento river, the myths obtained there would seem to represent the valley half of this division. The tales from the northeastern and northwestern divisions are given intermingled by Dr. Dixon, though always with indication of the place of origin of each story. In spite of the greater incompleteness of the Chico or northwestern series, it parallels the northeastern, so that the character common to both is perhaps brought out more strongly by considering them separately; and this will here be done.

The northeastern Maidu series, though the fuller, is represented by a creation myth, number 2, that is either incomplete or less typical than the northwestern one given by Dr. Dixon. The principal character, Earth-namer or Earth-maker, plays the part of a transformer rather than of an actual creator. The origin of the physical world is also not accounted for by the myth. The relation of the transformer-creator to Coyote, and the conceptions displayed as to the destiny of man, however, affiliate this northeastern myth with the northwestern one. A version of this myth by Powers, mentioned below, amplifies the present one by narrating also the creation of men from sticks.[5] The next most important northeastern Maidu tale, that of the conqueror, number 3, tells of a supernaturally born destroyer, conqueror, and avenger. After recounting the origin of this hero, the myth consists of a series of detached incidents of adventure, all more or less of the same nature. Next follows the account of the theft of fire from its original owner, number 5. The story of Thunder and his daughter, number 6, has for its essence the successful escape of the hero from dangers caused by his father-in-law, whom he finally overcomes. This type of myth is one of the most favored, not only, as will be seen, in this region of California, but in other parts of North America, such as the Plains and the North Pacific Coast. The story of the Loon-woman, number 7, is apparently confined to a circumscribed region in northern California, but within this is quite typical. Its fundamental idea, that of love between a brother and sister , has equivalents in the mythology of most tribes on the continent of North America. In northern California Curtin gives this particular Loon-woman form from the Yana, and Dr. Dixon mentions it as found among the Achomawi. It occurs also among the Karok of northwestern California. The story of the sun and moon, number 8, first part, has for its chief episode a conflict between the sun and the frog. The tale of the bear and deer children, number 9, is, as noted by Dr. Dixon, a great favorite in northern California. The bear kills the deer; the deer children kill the bear children, flee, and finally escape the pursuing bear. It will be seen below that this story is found also in certain parts of south central California; and it occurs among at least some of the tribes of northwestern California. Within these limits, although frequently connected with distinct and unrelated episodes, it shows everywhere fundamentally the same form. Moreover this tale is one of the few characteristic of California and found also outside the state." A number of short Coyote stories given by Dr. Dixon, number 10, 1-7, 16., are similar to the Coyote and trickster stories found in a generally similar form everywhere in North America. In a number of these from the northeastern Maidu there is a contest between Coyote and an opponent. Sometimes Coyote is superior and sometimes he is worsted. The story of the woman who falls in love with the butterflies, number 12, seems quite specialized. The tale of the Frog-woman who acts the impostor for another woman, number 13, rests on an idea found elsewhere; but the association of the frog with this incident is quite typical of northern California. The tale of the lizard and the grizzly bear, number 16, is an animal tale of a certain simplicity. The grizzly bear having killed all the lizard's relatives except him and his grandmother, the lizard in revenge first reviles and then kills the bear. As will be seen, this story is paralleled in south central California. The several northeastern Maidu stories of the fish-hawk and the deer ticks, of the skunk and the beetle, and of the wolf making the snow cold, numbers 11, 17, 18, are comparatively trivial and humorous. In the tale of Big-belly's son, number 21, the essential element is again the idea of the revenging hero. In addition, the deceitful Frog-woman again appears. The story of the mountain lion, who deserts his wives, whereupon his children support themselves until they induce their father to return, number 22, has only general parallels in south central California and on the Plains. So far the northeastern Maidu stories.

The northwestern Maidu myths begin with a fully developed and typical creation myth, number 1. In the beginning everything is water. The creator descends from the sky and makes earth from mud for which the turtle has dived. He brings forth the sun and moon and makes the stars. He makes animals, makes people, and vivifies them. He fails, owing to Coyote's opposition, in making men immortal. Coyote suffers in the death of his own son for being responsible for bringing death into the world. Men come to speak different languages, and Kuksu, the first man, sends away the tribes with directions as to their life and customs. After this account of the creation, the next most important northwestern myth, number 4, is an exact parallel, in its general course, to the northeastern conqueror story, although the individual incidents mostly differ. Several Coyote tales, number 10, 10-15, are given. The first of these relates the theft of fire; the next, like a number from the northeastern Maidu, tells of contests of Coyote in which he is sometimes superior and sometimes inferior; and several other Coyote tales develop incidents of the well-known and wide-spread type of unsuccessful imitation. The story of the devouring head, number 14, is found in some form, and in a great many different connections, over the larger part of North America. The particular form that occurs here appears also among the neighboring Yana. The story of the stolen brother who was taken to the sky and finally recovered, number 15, has a number of parallels in northern California. Curtin gives a Wintun version and another was obtained by the author among the Salmon river Shasta. Similar mythical ideas, sometimes with the visit to the sky forming the principal feature and sometimes with this omitted, are found farther north on the Pacific Coast and to the east. The northwestern story of Thunder and his daughter, number 19, is perhaps a modified form of the evil father-in-law tale. At any rate it connects with it in being similar to the northeastern story of Thunder and his daughter, which belongs clearly to this type.

Several Maidu myths given by Stephen Powers,[6] while not forming a systematic collection, supplement Dr. Dixon's in a very satisfactory fashion. Powers distinguishes between the Maidu, corresponding to Dixon's northeastern and northwes-tern Maidu, and the Nishinam, who are Dixon's southern Maidu. From the former he gives the Kodoyanpe or creator and Onkoito or conqueror myths, in versions agreeing closely with

Dixon's northeastern forms and in part amplifying them. A story of which the wild-cat is the hero, an animal myth of a younger brother[7] who succeeds through magical power, is not given by Dr. Dixon. Powers' southern Maidu myths are particularly valuable. One tells of the causation of death and cremation by Coyote, who argues against a return of man to life and prevails. When his own son is killed by a rattlesnake, Coyote is unable to undo his decision. In another story Coyote appears as the destroyer, by deceit, of a cannibal. In another tale, the theft of fire which is accomplished by the lizard results in a general conflagration. The bear and deer story is another one given.

That of Aitut and Yototowi is interesting because it is a version of the tale of the visit to the dead characteristic of the San Joaquin valley. This is its northernmost occurrence known. This circumstance, and the fact that no creation myth is given by Powers, point to some mythological relationship of the southern Maidu with their neighbors the Miwok, corroborating Dr. Dixon's statements as to their culture in general.

Wintun

Curtin's "Creation Myths of Primitive America" contains twenty-two tales, the first nine from the Wintun, the last thirteen from the Yana. The last of the Wintun stories is not a myth. The Wintun tales are told at great length, and therefore more than make up for their small number. They are all from the northern Wintun, apparently not far from the Shasta region; and as the Wintun family has a long narrow north and south distribution, Curtin's myths must not be regarded as typical of the entire stock.[8] There is every reason to believe from the general cultural relations that the mythology of the southernmost Wintun was nearer to that of the Pomo, and perhaps other adjacent groups, than to the northern Wintun material given by

Curtin. In their form also Curtin's Wintun myths cannot be considered as typical of the character of the mythology of a large area any more than in their locality. It would appear from their general similarity that they may all have been obtained from a single individual of unusual power, not only of narration, but of mythological combination; and it is likely that the same tales as told by the majority of the Wintun of the region may have been much less developed both in detail and in arrangement. Finally, the systematization of this mythology as set forth in the author's introduction and notes must be kept carefully apart from the systematization actually present in the myths themselves.

The northern Wintun conception of Olelbis, "sitting in the above" or "he who is in heaven," shows a developed and a lofty conception of a creator. At the same time it is very noticeable that creation takes place not so much by actual making or calling into existence on the part of the supreme deity, as is the case among the Maidu, as by the origination of objects and faculties from a number of individual beings distinct from him and already endowed with certain powers. The water woman is the originator of water, the child of the fire-drill of fire, Old-man white-oak-acorn of oak trees, the cloud dogs of clouds. Similar characters are Wind, and Katkatchila, the "swift," from whom flint was obtained for the people of the world. The principal incidents of the long Olelbis myth, given in sequence rather than in the order of Curtin, are as follows:

Olelbis makes a great sweat-house in the sky with the help of two old women whom he calls his grandmothers. People steal flint from its possessor. In revenge he causes a world fire. Olelbis has Water-woman put it out. The earth being then bare, earth is brought on it and the mountains are made. This is done by order of Olelbis, but it is to be noted that the earth with which the world is covered, is not made by him but is found beyond the confines of the human world. Fire is obtained from the fire people by theft, though without the pursuit usually narrated in American myths of the theft of fire. Then rivers are made by Olelbis. The fish in them, however, spring from one fish left in a pool of water after the world fire and world flood. Then oaks are made through the power of Old-man-acorn. Deer, elk, shells, and other objects entering into Indian life are made from portions of the body of Wokwuk, a mythical bird with Olelbis. The cloud dogs are caught by Olelbis and the clouds made of their skins. Then Olelbis sends off the various people of the world of that time, each with his specific qualities, to turn into animals and inanimate objects.

After this creation myth are told the following stories.

In the second, Water-woman, here the wife of Olelbis, is carried off by Wind. Water is reobtained from her.

In the third story, a woman called Norwan, of supernatural origin, is married, and, upon her deserting her husband at a dance, a battle occurs. The remainder of this long tale is filled with accounts of fighting of an epic character, three battles taking place altogether.

The fourth story, that of Tulchuherris, tells of the hero who is dug from the ground, a common conception both in northwestern and central California as well as elsewhere in America. In body, this myth belongs to the class telling of the successful overcoming by the hero of his evil father-in-law, who in this case is the sun. A number of the incidents, such as that of the swinging on a tree with the object of dashing the opponent against the sky, are favorites in north central as well as northwestern California.

The fifth story, that of Coyote and the buzzards, tells of the origin of death. Its form is quite philosophical, but the ideas it embodies are found throughout central California, and almost invariably associated with Coyote.

The sixth tale, that of Hawt, is one of character and supernatural powers rather than of plot or incidents. The hero is the lamprey eel.

The seventh story, that of Norwanchakus and Keriha, contains three principal and really distinct portions. The first narrates the theft of daylight, an idea found also among the coast Indians of northern California. The second is a contest of Keriha with the wasp. In the third part of the tale, Keriha, the younger brother, is stolen. His location is learned from the sun. The people then climb to the sky and he is rescued. This mythical idea has been mentioned in connection with the northwestern Maidu.

The eighth myth, that of wolf and Coyote, is again one of character rather than of plot. Coyote is inferior to the being whom he imitates. The making of persons from sticks, a common California conception, is also told.

A southern Wintun myth from middle Cache creek given by Stephen Powers' tells of a world conflagration started in anger, of its burning southward, of its extinction by Coyote, who thereupon also renews water, and of his creation of people from sticks. There is sufficient here to show that the northern Wintun Olelbis myth is not without some parallels in the southern part of the family; but the creator himself is replaced by Coyote. Dixon[9] mentions that among the southern Wintun there is little antithesis between creator and Coyote in the creation myth, and that the story of the theft of fire resembles the northern Maidu version more closely than does the northern Wintun one.

Yana

Curtin's Yana myths, though more numerous than his Wintun ones, are less distinctive. They represent evidently only part of the mythology of the tribe, for no creation myth is given. The last myth in the book has as its concluding incident the making of man from sticks, but only as an episode, and undoubtedly does not adequately represent the ideas of the Yana as to the creation. Most of the thirteen stories, and a great many of the episodes contained in them, have parallels among the Maidu or Wintun or both. The sixteenth story tells of the theft of fire. The contest of the hero with his father-in-law, and his final victory over him, are told in two stories, the tenth and twentieth. The eleventh story, that of the Hakas and the Tennas, the flints and the grizzly bears, and the twelfth, that of Ilhataina, tell of the revenge taken by the hero upon those who have destroyed his people. The hero of the latter tale has his origin by being dug out of the ground. The thirteenth tale, that of Hitchinna, is the familiar one of the rolling devouring head. The nineteenth, called that of the two sisters, is the loon-woman story that has been commented upon in connection with the Maidu. The incident of the frog-women acting as substitutes or imposters is found in the fifteenth story, that of Sukonia's wives. The remaining tales have little specific character, but are stories of fighting, fleeing from monsters, overcoming of dangers, and victory in gambling, with the supernatural and magical element strongly developed and at times rather extravagant. While the Yana material given by Curtin is not sufficient to allow of a statement of what elements that are found among neighboring tribes their mythology lacks; yet it is evident, if this material is at all typical, that the Yana mythology contains probably no very important ideas that are specific to it and foreign to the Wintun and Maidu.

Dr. Dixon has collected myths among the Yana, but they are as yet unpublished. In the course of a general discussion he mentions the general close similarity between Yana, Achomawi, and northern Maidu mythologies. In regard to the creation--where Curtin's published material is deficient--he states that the Yana told of a primeval water, and of constant difference of purpose between the creator and Coyote. The Yana story of the theft of fire as outlined by Dr. Dixon differs from that told by Curtin. It is discovered mainly by the lizard, and the pursuers are hindered by having their dresses cut while asleep. According to Dr. Dixon, the bear and deer children story also belongs to the Yana.[10]

Shasta-Achomawi

The mythology of the Achomawi or Pit River Indians, north of the Maidu, is nearly unknown. Powers[11] has a paragraph on their creation myth. Coyote made the earth by scratching it out of nothingness. The eagle continued and made the mountains. The eagle's feathers turned to vegetation--an idea with Wintun and Yuki parallels. Coyote and the fox made men; the former, after a dispute, prevailed and caused permanent death. Coyote stole fire. Dr. Dixon[12] states that the Achomawi tell the creation of men much like the northwestern Maidu: Coyote attempts to imitate the creator and makes deformed people through not restraining himself. Elsewhere[13] he says that the Achomawi account of the beginning of the world is similar to the Maidu one, but carries the origin back farther. A cloud forms and grows into the silver-gray fox, the creator. Then Coyote is formed. By thought the creator makes a canoe in which the two remain until they make the world. The antithesis between them is similar to that in Maidu creation myths. Altogether, according to Dr. Dixon, the mythology of the Achomawi and that of the northern Maidu and the Yana is much alike. A special form of the theft of fire and of the loon-woman myth has been found so far only among them; and in other tales, such as those of the bear and deer children, the sisters sent to marry the stranger, and the Coyote stories, there is also close similarity.

Of the mythology of the Shasta, Dr. Dixon says[14] that the creation myth is brief, undeveloped, and of a different type from that of the Maidu, Coyote being the creator as well as the trickster. He mentions a story of the theft of fire different from the characteristic version of the northern Maidu, Yana, and Achomawi, and says that the Shasta also tell the Loon-woman myth in a modified form.

Half a dozen Scott's Valley Shasta myths told by L. M. Burns[15] deal mostly with Coyote and contain no approach to a creation myth. One tells of the theft of fire by Coyote. In the others he is a trickster, usually coming out inferior. One tale is a version of the imposter frog-woman. The last of the myths has a dug-from-the-ground hero and belongs to the evil father-in-law type, with numerous analogues in northern California. There is also a version of the story of the actions of panther, wild-cat, and Coyote in connection with the supernatural control of the deer. This myth having been found also among the Maidu, Yuki, and Lassik, appears to be of general distribution in the northern Central region. The Shasta form agrees with the Maidu in making the wild-cat the recoverer of a magic ball controlling deer, whereas in the Yuki and Lassik versions he causes the loss of the power by yielding to Coyote.

Several Shasta myths collected by the author on Salmon river[16] also include no creation myth or mention of a creator. One of them gives the origin of death. The cricket's child dying, Coyote refuses to let it live again. Later his own child dies. Fire is stolen from across the ocean by the bluejay, robin, turtle, and ground-squirrel. They bring with them also acorns. There are northwestern resemblances in this myth. A fragment which tells how Coyote tried to make the white deer-skin dance near Sawyer's Bar on the north fork of the Salmon, but found the place too narrow; then tried Forks of Salmon; and finally the mouth of the Salmon, where the Karok actually make the ceremony; is distinctly northwestern in spirit. So is a story of a hero--from Karok territory--who was rejected by two sisters when he appeared covered with sores, but was accepted when the sores changed to woodpecker scalps, and who played shinny with the ten thunder brothers and beat them. A tale of a girl who turns to a devouring bear has many parallels in the interior of the continent. A story of the evil father-in-law, in this case the sun, and one of the brother who was stolen and recovered from the sky, are of north central California type, and of considerable similarity to Curtin's northern Wintun versions. Altogether the Salmon Shasta seem to have been under greater Karok influence than the main body of the stock farther east; this is natural, as they lived only a few miles from some of the most important places held by the Karok.

The absence of a true creator from Shasta mythology must not be regarded as necessarily all approximation to northwestern beliefs, for there are as yet no evidences of any Shasta equivalents of the characteristic northwestern culture-heroes.[17]

Lutuami

The myths of the Lutuami, the Klamath Lake and Modoc Indians, who were on the whole inhabitants of Oregon rather than of California, are in part recorded in Gatschet's Klamath Indians of Southwestern Oregon;[18] but a much larger body of material that has been secured is still unpublished.[19] Lutuami mythology is quite unlike that of central California. The bear and deer children story occurs, but the general character of the mythology is much more reminiscent of the North Pacific Coast and the interior of North America, and in part directly of north-western California. There is a creator, K'mukamtch, old man, but he is not the "good" creator of the Maidu, Wintun, Yuki, and Wishosk; he is deceitful, with the character of the typical culture-hero-trickster. His relation to his son Aishish, including a number of specific incidents, can be paralleled among the Indians of northwestern California, who, it should be remembered, live on the lower drainage of the river system of which the Lutuami hold the headwaters. The central California opposition between creator and Coyote is lacking, although Coyote occurs in many typical "Coyote-stories." The reduction by K'mukamtch of the female Coyote's twenty-four, and therefore unendurable, moons to twelve, shows perhaps a faint approximation to this antithesis. The origin of death from the wish of the mole and an insect, Coyote not being concerned in the matter, has parallels in northwestern California. Next to the K'mukamtch cycle, the most important series of Lutuami myths appears to be that of Marten, sometimes identified with K'mukamtch, and his younger brother Weasel. Marten is a trickster and destroyer; the point of his achievements is not so much the benefit resulting to the world from his riddance of it from evils, as the means of his superiority over them. He therefore corresponds more to the Manabozho and North Pacific Coast culture-hero type than to the Maidu Conqueror. Even in details,--the creation of man, the thunders, the firing of the sky, the failures of the trickster,--there are few Central Californian resemblances, but a number to the other culture regions mentioned. While the known Lutuami myth material is unfortunately very limited as compared with that which has been collected, it is sufficient to show that mythologically these people stood outside the Central Californian cultural type.

Yuki

The Yuki are the first northern California people, of those so far discussed, the Coast Range instead of the Sacramento Valley or Sierra Nevada region. No account of their mythology has been published, but a summary is here given from material collected by the author. The creator and supreme deity of the Yuki is Taikomol, "He who goes alone." The usual antithetical relation of Coyote to the creator occurs, although on the whole Coyote's part is supplementary, rather than opposed, to that of the creator. The creation myth is long and contains many episodes that have little organic connection; so that the order of these varies in different versions, and sometimes even as told by the same narrator; but the episodes themselves are told with more uniformity.

In the beginning everything was water. On the water, in a fleck of foam, a down feather was circling. From this issued a voice and singing. This was the creator, Taikomol. Coyote is represented as being present, though in what form or resting on what is not told, and as seeing the birth or self-creation of Taikomol. The creator addresses him throughout as "mother's brother;" but this seems not to imply any conception of actual relationship between them, as mother's brother is the regular term of address used by all myth-beings for Coyote. He as regularly calls them "my sister's child." The creator after a time gradually assumes human physical shape, all the time singing and watched by Coyote. He thereupon forms the earth from a piece of coiled basket which he makes of materials and with an awl that he takes from his body. The earth is fastened and strengthened with pitch, and the creator thereupon travels over it four times from north to south with Coyote hanging to his body. He then fastens the earth at the four ends and makes the sky from the skin of four whales. After this he marries his sister, whose origin is not related and who is not mentioned again, and thus institutes cohabitation. Thereupon he makes people, according to a frequent Californian conception from sticks laid in the house over night, in the morning these sticks arise as people. Then follows a journey to the north, in which Coyote accompanies the creator, who, it is said, marries there. On the return, death is brought into the world through the instrumentality of Coyote, whose son dies and is buried by him. Taikomol offers to restore him to life, but Coyote insists that the dead shall remain dead. Then follows a long journey of the creator, still accompanied by Coyote, in the course of which he makes tribes in different localities, in each case by laying sticks in the house over night, gives them their customs and mode of life, and each their language. In some versions two episodes are made of these incidents. After this the creator makes mountains, springs, and streams, mainly from condor feathers. He then either makes, or, according to another account, instructs Coyote to make, the first ceremonies. Sometimes Coyote is represented as at first making the supernatural power of these ceremonies so strong that the human participants die in the course of them, whereupon the creator modifies them. The creator then journeys westward across the ocean to visit his sister, who, it is said, is not the one previously mentioned. He arranges for his brother to stand at the end of the world during summer and his sister during winter. Finally, having returned to this world, he ascends to the sky; and there he still is.

This creation myth is followed by a long Coyote culture-hero myth. The principal episodes that have been obtained in this are the following. The people, through the intelligence of Coyote and with him as helper, obtain fire by theft from the spider, who alone has kept it. Coyote leads a successful war expedition against a northern tribe by which visiting Yuki have been killed. He supernaturally learns of the existence of the sun, visits the people who keep it, steals it, and flees. He is killed, but succeeds in returning to life and escaping with the sun. He makes another journey, and, through the stratagem of assuming the shape of a woman, steals the moon and the morning-star. Having again been killed by the pursuers and returned to life, he thereupon causes the heavenly bodies to rise and fixes their courses. Another journey is made by him to the people who keep acorns, seeds, and other foods, and results in the acquisition of these for the people. According to one account he then makes people, as the creator is previously represented as having done; but through the lizard they are given a five-fingered hand instead of the fist with which Coyote had first provided them. Finally Coyote sends off the people of the world of that time to become animals, directing each with what qualities and in what manner to live.

The Yuki myths less directly connected than the foregoing with creation and the origin of culture, have not been obtained so completely. There appear to be numerous stories in which Coyote appears in a ridiculous character. There are also hero, adventure, and animal stories of the types found elsewhere in California. Perhaps the most important of these is a myth of the twins Burnt-sling and Hummingbird. These two boys, being dirty, are repudiated by their parents, and live with their grandmother. They develop great supernatural powers. Going out to hunt crickets, they make springs of water. When hunting butterflies, they kill condors in the sky. They are attacked by war parties from the north, and kill them by waving a supernatural wand. Other enemies that come against them from the north are killed with their slings. With these they shoot gaps and valleys into the mountains. With their slings they also break the sky, which is supported, and then repaired, by their grandmother the mole. They kill their evil parents, turning their father into harmless thunder. They make a lake, and, to terrify their grandmother, catch water monsters. Finally they travel north. They reach people who habitually kill some of their own number as if they were deer and then eat them. They teach these people to kill real deer and to eat human food. Finally the twins go to the sky. Of other Yuki stories a favorite tells of the wild-cat, the son of the panther. Coyote comes in the absence of the boy's elder brothers, persuades him to show how the deer are supernaturally brought, and kills one. The angered older brothers kill the wild-cat by burning him, but he is brought back to life.[20]

MYTHOLOGY OF THE SOUTHERN CENTRAL REGION

While the northern half of the Central ethnological region of California is represented by collections of myths sufficiently numerous and large to allow of an estimate of the essential character of the mythology of this area, conditions are very different in the southern half of the same culture region. There is not a single noteworthy collection of native traditions from the entire territory extending from San Francisco and Sacramento on the north to Tehachapi on the south, a full third of the state. Four entire linguistic stocks, the Costanoan, Esselen, Salinan, and Yokuts, and parts of two others, the Miwok and Shoshonean, were embraced in this territory. A number of myths, singly and in small groups, have been published from various parts of this region, but they are neither numerous nor extensive, and some are not of much value.

Stephen Powers gives a few bits of mythology from the Miwok, the Yokuts, and the Shoshoneans of the San Joaquin valley.[21] His Miwok account of the creation shows little except the consequence, in the beliefs of these people, of Coyote, who is the creator of man. Powers' other Miwok stories are of small value for purposes of comparison, being local legends referring to Yosemite. He gives one Yokuts story,--it is not stated from what locality,--which resembles one of the Yokuts versions of creation presented in this paper. At first, according to this account, there was only water, from which a "pole" stood up. On this were the hawk and the crow. These made various birds. Of these birds the duck dived and brought up earth from the bottom of the water. From this the world was made. Thereupon the hawk and crow made mountains of earth, the hawk the Sierra Nevada, the crow the Coast Range. The crow stole part of the, hawk's earth and therefore made his range the largest. The hawk, on discovering the trickery, interchanged the mountains, so that the Sierra Nevada is now higher than the Coast Range. In essentials this story appears to be a correct representation of the creation myth of one of the Yokuts tribes. The Shoshonean myth material. given by Powers is fragmentary and slight.

A number of Indian myths and traditions referring to Yosemite have been published in various connections.' Most of these are of the usual character of Indian local legends as they are commonly imagined and sometimes invented by the whites. Some others are more accurate, but as even the best have been obtained not with any idea of illustrating the life or thought of the Indians, but from narrower interests, they are unrepresentative of the general beliefs of the Indians.

Dr. J. W. Hudson has published 2 two versions of "In Indian Myth of the San Joaquin Basin,"--the visit to the dead of the dead in pursuit of a wife,--one version from the southern and the other from the northern part of Yokuts territory. This myth has close parallels in two versions presented in this paper. One of these, number 31, may have been obtained from the same informant as Dr. Hudson's Tule river version. He states that this story is found also among the Miwok; and, it will be recalled, Powers gives a southern Maidu version mentioned above.

Bancroft quotes from the Hesperian Magazine,[22] from an author who signs himself only with the initials H. B. D., a myth the tribe or location or which is not stated, but which is of considerable importance because it is perhaps from the northern part of the Costanoan territory. The entire world, it is said, except the summits of Mt. Diablo and Reed Peak, was covered with water. Coyote was alone on the latter peak. A feather floated on the water. This turned to an eagle who joined Coyote. The two then sometimes went from one peak to the other. They created men, and the water abated. At first there were only two streams, Russian river and the San Juan (sic). Later the Golden Gate was formed and the San Joaquin and Sacramento rivers began to flow through it. The last part of this story is somewhat suspicious on account of the notions of geography that it introduces, as it is doubtful whether any Indian tribe of central California had knowledge of so extensive a tract of country as is implied. The first part of the story is however undoubtedly correct, and bears a close resemblance to the Costanoan creation myth given in this paper. The eagle appears as the leading one of the creators not only in the Costanoan but in the Miwok and Yokuts myths obtained by the author. His origin from a feather floating on the water is similar to the Yuki origin of the creator.

In the "History of Washington Township, Alameda County,"[23] is given a tradition of the Indians attached to Mission San Jose, relating the origin of death. While this mission was in Costanoan territory and many of its Indians were Costanoan, Indians of other families were also brought to it. Most of the surviving Indians, now at Pleasanton and Niles, who were formerly at Mission San Jose, are Miwok. It is therefore uncertain whether this myth is Miwok or Costanoan. As given it relates that a woman lay in a trance and no one was to make a sound for four days. The lark, however, sang. The girl died and in consequence all people die. To-day when Indians kill a lark they strike its bill and say: "If you had not spoken we should not die." It will be seen that this tradition of the origin of death resembles, one from the Southern Miwok given in this paper.

In the same connection is mentioned an annual dance held by the San Jose Indians in September. Part of this was the Coyote dance, a rude sort of play, in which one of the favorite characters was Cooksuy, a clown. This dance was said to have been made on account of the dead. The reference to Cooksuy allies the mythology of the people performing this dance, whoever they may have been, to the mythologies of northern central California. Among many of the Pomo, Wintun, Maidu, and perhaps Indians of other families, Kuksu is a personage of some mythological prominence and great ceremonial importance. It is very unusual in California to find a mythological or ceremonial name maintaining itself beyond the limits of a single linguistic family. The present reference shows that the name and conception of Kuksu evidently extended beyond the southern Sacramento valley and adjacent coast region to the region south, either in the. Sierra Nevada or on the coast.

A sentence written by Alexander Taylor[24] about the mythology of the Indians of Mission San Antonio, who are of Salinan family, is of particular importance. It shows the ideas of creation of these Indians to have been similar to those presented in this paper from the Costanoan Indians of Monterey. Taylor says that "one of their superstitions was that the humming bird was first brother of the coyote, and he was first brother to the eagle." This statement appears to contain absolutely all that is known of the mythology of the Salinan stock.

A Wükchamni Yokuts myth recently contributed to the Journal of American Folk-Lore by Mr. George W. Stewart of Visalia supplements a creation myth given in this paper from the same tribe, number 25. The world being without fire, the wolf, at the bidding of his brother Coyote, obtains some in the mountains, from which Coyote makes sun and moon. Coyote, under the direction of the eagle, and with the help of wolf and panther, makes streams, game, fish, and people. The people increase so that the creators leave and go to the sky, mountains, and plains; that is to say, become transformed to animals.

The myths here presented from south-central California were obtained, as stated, in the course of various investigations connected with the Ethnological and Archaeological Survey of California, and belong to Indians of the Costanoan, Miwok, Yokuts, and Shoshonean families.

Costanoan

The Costanoan myths are nothing but fragments, except for the creation myth, and this is brief. They are, however, perhaps the most important of all that are given, because of our almost complete ignorance of the ethnology of. these people and the slenderness of the prospect that much more material can be obtained. The numerous village communities of the Costanoan family, once extending from San Francisco to Monterey, and from the ocean to the San Joaquin river, have shrunk to a few dozen persons, all of them entirely civilized and living, as equals, among, the Mexican population of this region. The stories obtained were told in Monterey by two old women, Jacinta Gonzalez and Maria Viviena Soto. They include an origin myth, in which a trinity consisting of the eagle, the humming bird, and the coyote are the creators, and which begins with universal water, but with the creators on a mountain top instead of on a raft as among the Maidu, or on a tree as among the Yokuts. The diving for the earth is in consequence not told. The remaining stories all relate to Coyote. In the first he appears as the giver of culture to the people; it is evident that his part in Costanoan mythology was important. The other tales or fragments dealing with him are typical Coyote stories, and have no reference to origins.

Miwok

The few Miwok stories given were obtained in the course of investigations among the northernmost Yokuts. They were told by two men living among the Chukchansi of Madera county, Bill White and Captain Charlie. Both of these men were half Pohonichi Miwok and half Yokuts in descent. The humming-bird of the Costanoan people disappears as a creator among the Miwok. The eagle is mentioned as chief in mythical times, but, at least in the stories told, about everything of consequence connected with creation is performed by Coyote. The Miwok creation myth mentioned as given by Powers is from a more northerly portion of the stock than that represented in the present paper, but shows Coyote in the same important role. The existence of primeval water, and a diving for the earth from which the world is made, are the only incidents contained in the fragment that was obtained by the author. A second story tells of the theft of fire by Coyote; and a third of the origin of death in connection with though not through him. All these ideas are typical of almost all parts of central California. It is illuminating that the fourth myth given, the. only one obtained not dealing with creation, is that of the bear and deer children.

Yokuts

The Yokuts myths, numbers 11 to 40, make up the bulk of this paper. They were obtained from individuals belonging to several tribes and in part are attributed by them to still other tribes.

The first four of these myths are from the Gashowu, now living south of the San Joaquin a few miles above Pollasky. They were obtained from a young man called Guadalupe and a blind old man named Bill. The account of the creation contains the ideas of the diving for the earth and the making and interchange of the mountains which are narrated also by other Yokuts. The version of the origin of death resembles that of the Pohonichi Miwok. Number 14, the longest of the Gashowu tales, is evidently a composite. Two of the elements composing it have not yet been found elsewhere in south central California, but are Paralleled among distant tribes. These are the marriage of Coyote to the woman with the rattlesnake, which has analogues, especially on the North Pacific Coast as far down as northwestern California, and the episode of the people who were so constructed that they could not eat, which has an Eskimo equivalent from Baffin Land.

The next ten of the Yokuts stories, numbers 15 to 24, were obtained from a man named Tom belonging to the Tachi. This tribe lived at the northern end of Tulare lake. The first four of these myths were stated by the informant not to belong to his people but to be stories of the Truhohi, a tribe mentioned also as Truhohayi or Tukhokhayi by other Indian informants, and now extinct. They inhabited the region near the southern end of Tulare lake. The principal origin stories told by this informant are among these four attributed to the Truhohi. The account of the making of the earth and mountains resembles that given by the Gashowu and the version told by Powers. Other of the Truhohi stories tell of the origin of fire, mainly through the instrumentality of Coyote; of the origin of death, for which, however, Coyote is not responsible; and of the origin of the sun. The remaining six stories of this group of ten are apparently true Tachi, and include an account of the origin of the milky way from a race of the antelope and the deer, a story which is interesting on account of the close parallel that it furnishes to myths of the Indians of the Plains; two other star myths, including one about the Pleiades; a story in which the prairie falcon figures as hero; a tale about twins of miraculous power, connected here, as often elsewhere in California, with thunder; and a typical version of the visit to the dead.

The following twelve stories, numbers 25 to 36, were obtained from Peter Christman, an Indian of the Yaudanchi or original Tule river tribe. This informant was not acquainted with the creation myth of his own people, but narrated a Wükchamni version which he had learned from a man named Jo living on the same reservation. The Wükchamni were a Kaweah river tribe just north of the Yaudanchi and spoke an almost identical dialect. The story of Mikiti, number 34, also seems not to be Yaudanchi. It is stated by the informant to have been learned by him from a man who was a Yauelmani Yokuts. The localities mentioned are, however, in the territory of the Paleuyami tribe, and is not unlikely that the myth belongs to these people. This is a story resembling some found among the Sacramento valley tribes, for instance Curtin's Yana myth of the Hakas and the Tennas. The hero, a boy, is brought up by his grandmother and kills those who have destroyed his relatives. The remaining stories of this group are apparently Yaudanchi. There is a version of the theft of fire, which is, however, accomplished by the rabbit, not by Coyote. Most of the stories deal either with the eagle or the prairie falcon. There is also a version of the visit to the dead.

The Yauelmani stories given, numbers 37 to 40, are from two informants, both on Tule river reservation. The original territory of the Yauelmani was south of Tule river, apparently about Kern river in the vicinity of Bakersfield and above to Gonoilkin. Number 37 was obtained from Cow, the oldest man on the reservation, and is a somewhat fuller account of the creation, with the usual prominence of the eagle and Coyote and the episode of the diving for the earth, than any of the other Yokuts versions obtained. The antithesis between the wolf and Coyote is interesting because it reappears in other parts of California.

The dignity of character attributed to the prairie falcon is also noticeable. The following fragment, number 38, from the same informant, shows Coyote as the cause of death, and is interesting because it reveals the presence among these people of the wide-spread Californian belief of the origin of the human hand as patterned upon that of the lizard. The next two stories, numbers 39 and 40, were obtained from an informant named Chalola, also an old man. The first of these two is by far the longest myth in the entire collection, and appears to consist of three more or less separate series of incidents. It is doubtful how far the joining together of these is due to the individual narrator. The first part tells how Coyote caused the absence of the sun in order to avenge himself upon the people with whom he lived. In this part of the myth he is the hero. The second portion is much more loosely put together, and consists of a string of typical Coyote episodes, his character being throughout ridiculous. A sudden transition made from Coyote to the prairie falcon, leads to the third portion of this myth, which tells of the prairie falcon's loss of his eyes in gambling and his travels. This part of the story seems to be little else than a framework for a number of songs. The second Yauelmani story obtained from this informant, number 40, is also of some length and again has the prairie falcon as its hero.

Shoshonean

Only one Shoshonean myth is given, the last in the collection. This is from the Gitanemuk or Gikidanum, a tribe on upper Tejon creek at the extreme southern end of the San Joaquin valley. Linguistically the Gitanemuk are very closely related to the Serrano of the San Bernardino mountains in Southern California. This story was obtained from the same Yauelmani informant, Chalola, who had lived for many years among the Gitanemuk. This one myth is not of a character to give any indication as to the general nature of the beliefs of the people to whom it belongs. It is apparently the first myth published not only from this tribe but from any of the Shoshonean groups of the southern San Joaquin-Tulare basin.

General Characterization

From this new material the mythological beliefs of three of the linguistic families of South central California, the Costanoan, the Miwok, and the Yokuts, can be summarized and compared as follows with the beliefs of the Indians of northern Central California.

Among the Costanoan Indians the eagle, the humming-bird, Coyote are the creators. The eagle is the chief, the humming-bird the favorite, and Coyote both an object of ridicule and the originator of culture for the people. There is the general Californian conception of the origin of the world after a period of water; but the diving for the earth is not related.

The Miwok creation myths are characterized by the prominence of Coyote. The world begins with water, and the earth from which it is made is brought up by diving birds. Coyote seems to be responsible for most things, both in the physical world and in life of man. The presence, among the few myths collected from this people, of the bear and deer children story found throughout northern California, but not yet obtained among, the Yokuts to the south although a much larger body of myths was collected there, is perhaps indicative of a closer mythological relation of the Miwok to the north.

The Yokuts origin myths begin with water and a plurality of creators, of whom the eagle is the head. Coyote is also among them, and, while at times ridiculous in comparison with the others. is responsible for certain features of distinctively human life. There are stories of the theft of fire, and of the origin of death, which resemble those told in northern California. Hero stories recounting the miraculous origin of the hero and his numerous supernatural exploits, especially the destruction of monsters or rivals, appear to have been much less developed than in the Sacramento valley region. There is not one story that is clearly of this type among the twenty odd Yokuts myths obtained; whereas among the northern tribes such a tale is usually one of the most important next to the creation and culture myths. It is also noteworthy that the story of the evil father-in-law, which is so highly developed among the Maidu, Wintun, and Yana, is without a representative in the Yokuts collection. Instead of these type of myths, comparatively simple animal tales, without a very marked element of the supernatural, are found. In these the prairie falcon is a favorite hero. A mythological idea which has taken a special hold on the Yokuts is that of a man's visit to the world of the dead in pursuit of his wife.

COMPARISON OF THE MYTHOLOGIES OF NORTH AND SOUTH CENTRAL CALIFORNIA

Upon comparison, the several mythologies of the north and south halves of the Central ethnological region of California appear similar in the following respects: The possession of creation myths; the uniform antithesis, to a greater or less degree, of Coyote and the chief creator in these creation myths; the presence of numerous Coyote trickster stories; a considerable range of animal characters; certain ideas, also commonly held by the Indians of a large part of America, especially of the flood or primeval water, the theft of fire, and the origin of death, Coyote usually appearing in connection with the last two; and certain ideas of similar type which are more nearly confined to California, such as the origin of the human hand from the lizard in opposition to Coyote. In both north and south Central California there are no migration legends nor any long systematized myths giving the history of the people, of the type characterizing the Southwest and Southern California; nor is there a distinct culture-hero cycle such as is found almost everywhere on the Pacific Coast farther north than California; and finally, a well-developed idea of a previous race parallel to the present human race, but distinct from it in being the originators of things, is either wanting or much less clearly developed than in Northwestern California.

The following differences appear between the northern and southern halves of this Central region. In the south there are no developed or extensive creation myths. There is also scarcely a full creator. The eagle, who is most nearly such, is really only the chief among a number of equals. The mere fact that the creators are several, and that they are animals, must tend to minimize their distinctly creative qualities. Secondly, the hero stories and destroyer and transformer myths of the north are very little developed in the south. In place of the Maidu Conqueror, who destroys innumerable evils, the favorite hero of the San Joaquin valley Indians is the prairie falcon, who is represented as swift, silent, fierce, a successful gambler, and as living only on tobacco; but his exploits as compared with the startling and supernatural ones of the Maidu hero are such comparatively simple events as recovering his wife after she has been stolen, killing his enemies in battle, and losing his eyes in gambling. In this respect the simple Miwok and Tachi Yokuts stories of the supernatural Thunder twins are also typical of the south as com pared with the elaborate Yuki story of the twin children of Thunder. In the third place, episodes of magic are much less developed in the south than in the north, the stories being pitched throughout in a quieter and lower key. There are fewer fateful incidents dealing with life and death and involving supreme struggle and suspense. The tales are rather naïvely pleasant, with a semi-humorous element, and tell of but few contests except such as are more or less good-natured or peaceful. In a measure, of course, this contrast is due to the fact that the mythology of the south is, so far as collected, more broken under the influence of civilization than that of the north, and that in consequence aboriginal peculiarities and extravagances that once may have existed similar to those still found in the north, have now been lost or abbreviated. But after allowing for this factor it seems that a difference of tone must have existed between the two halves of the ethnic region even in former times. Among tales or incidents that occur in the north but seem to be either lacking or much less developed in the south or have not been found there, are the important story of the bear and deer children, which probably did not occur farther south than the Miwok; the equally important story dealing with the evil father-in-law, the peculiarly northern California story of the loon-woman; the story of the brother who ,vas stolen mid recovered from the sky; the impostor frog-woman; the devouring rolling head; and the hero who was dug from the ground. On the other hand the Indians of the northern half of the Central region show a different form of the story of the thunder twins, and lack entirely the peculiar southern Central conception of the character of the prairie falcon and the typical form of the tale of the visit to the dead.

RUMSIEN COSTANOAN. THE BEGINNING OF THE WORLD[25]

WHEN this world was finished, the eagle, the humming-bird, and Coyote were standing on the top of Pico Blanco. When the water rose to their feet, the eagle, carrying the humming-bird and Coyote, flew to the Sierra de Gabilan. There they stood until the water went down. Then the eagle sent Coyote down the mountain to see if the world were dry. Coyote came back and said: "The whole world is dry." The eagle said to him: "Go and look in the river. See what there is there." Coyote came back and said: "There is a beautiful girl." The eagle said: "She will be your wife in order that people may be raised again." He gave Coyote a digging implement of abalone shell and a digging stick. Coyote asked: "How will my children be raised'?" The eagle would not say. He wanted to sec if Coyote was wise enough to know. Coyote asked him again how these new people were to be raised from the girl. Then he said: "Well, I will make them right here in the knee." The eagle said: "No, that is not good." Then Coyote said: "Well then, here in the elbow." "No, that is not good" "In the eyebrow." "No, that is not good." "In the back of the neck." "No, that is not good either. None of these will be good." Then the humming-bird cried: "Yes, my brother, they are not good. This place will be good, here in the belly.- Then Coyote was angry. He wanted to kill him. The eagle raised his wings and the humming-bird flew in his armpit. Coyote, looked for him in vain. Then the girl said: "What shall I do? How will I make my children?" The eagle said to Coyote: "Go and marry her. She will be your wife." Then Coyote went off with this girl. He said to her: "Louse me." Then the girl found a woodtick on him. She was afraid and threw it away. Then Coyote seized her. He said: "Look for it, look for it! Take it! Eat it! Eat my louse!" Then the girl put it in her mouth. "'Swallow it, swallow it!" he said. Then she swallowed it and became pregnant. Then she was afraid. She ran away. She ran through thorns. Coyote ran after her. He called to her: "Do not run through that brush." He made a good road for her. But she said: "I do not like this road." Then Coyote made a road with flowers on each side. Perhaps the girl would stop to take a flower. She said. "I am not used to going between flowers." Then Coyote said: "There is no help for it. I cannot stop her." So she ran to the ocean. Coyote was close to her. Just as he was going to take hold of her, she threw herself into the water and the waves came up between them as she turned to a sand flea (or shrimp: camaron). Coyote, diving after her, struck only the sand. He said: "I wanted to clasp my wife but took hold of the sand. My wife is gone."

RUMSIEN COSTANOAN. COYOTE[26]

COYOTE'S wife said to him: "I do not want you to marry other women." Now they had only one child. Then Coyote said: "I want many children. We alone cannot have many children. Let me marry another woman so that there may be more of us." Then the woman said, "Well, go."

Then he had five children. Then his children said: "Where shall we make our houses? Where shall we marry?" Coyote told them: "Go out over the world." Then they went and founded five rancherias with five different languages. The rancherias are said to have been Ensen, Rumsien, Ekkheya, Kakonta, and that of the Wacharones.

Now Coyote gave the people the carrying net. He gave them bow and arrows to kill rabbits. He said: "You will have acorn mush for your food. You will gather acorns and you will have acorn bread to eat. Go down to the ocean and gather seaweed that you may eat it with your acorn mush and acorn bread. Gather it when the tide is low, and kill rabbits, and at low tide pick abalones and mussels to eat. When you can find nothing else, gather buckeyes for food. If the acorns are bitter, wash them out; and gather "wild oat" seeds for pinole, carrying them on your back in a basket. Look for these things of which I have told you. I have shown you what is good. Now I will leave you. You have learned. I have shown you how to gather food, and even though it rains a long time people will not die of hunger. Now I am getting old. I cannot walk. Alas for me! Now I go."

RUMSIEN COSTANOAN. COYOTE AND THE HUMMINGBIRD

COYOTE thought he knew more than anyone; but the hummingbird knew more. Then Coyote wanted to kill him. He caught him, struck him, and mashed him entirely. Then he went off. The hummingbird came to life, flew up, and cried: "Lakun, dead," in mockery. Coyote caught him, made a fire, and put him in. He and his people had gone only a little way when the hummingbird flew by crying: "Lakun!" Coyote said: "How shall I kill him?" They told him: "The only way is for you to eat him." Then Coyote swallowed him. The hummingbird scratched him inside. Coyote said: "What shall I do? I shall die." They said: "You must let him out by defecating." Then Coyote let him out and the hummingbird flew up crying: "Lakun!"

RUMSIEN COSTANOAN. COYOTE AND HIS WIFE

MAKEWIKS is an animal that lives in the ocean and sometimes comes to the surface. Coyote went to the ocean with his wife. He told her not to be afraid. He told her about the sea lion, about the mussels, about the crabs, and the octopus. He told her that all these were relatives; so when she saw them she was not afraid. But he did not tell her about the makewiks. Then when this rose before her it frightened her so that she fell dead. Coyote took her on his back, carried her off, built a fire, and laid her by the side of it. He began to sing and dance and jump. Soon she began to come to life. He jumped three times and brought her to life.

RUMSIEN COSTANOAN. COYOTE AND HIS CHILDREN

COYOTE killed salmon and put them into the ashes to roast. He did not want his children to eat them. Therefore he pretended that they where only ashes. Once in a while he reached into the ashes, took a piece, and ate it. Then his children cried out that he was eating fire and would be burned. When they wanted to take some, he did not let them. He said: "You will be burned."

RUMSIEN COSTANOAN. COYOTE WITH A THORN IN HIS EYE

COYOTE came to some women and asked them to pull out a thorn from his eye. There was only a little stick which he held in place with his eyelid. At first they distrusted him. He selected the most beautiful; "You draw it out," he sang. When she was about to take it with her fingers, he said: "No, take hold of it with your teeth." He said this so that he might seize her. When she took hold of the little stick he seized her and ran off with her. His song:

Meneya doñ kac op ka yapunnin, you (?) me pull-out my thorn!

POHONICHI MIWOK. THE BEGINNING OF THE WORLD

Told among the Chukchansi Yokuts

BEFORE there were people there was only water everywhere. Coyote looked among, the ducks and sent a certain species (Chukchansi: yimeit) to dive. It first it said it was unable to. Then it went down. It reached the bottom, bit the earth, and came up again. Coyote took the earth from it and sent it for chanit (Yokuts name) seeds. When the duck brought these he mixed them with the earth and water. Then the mixture swelled until the water had disappeared. The earth was there.

POHONICHI MIWOK. THE THEFT OF FIRE

Told among the Chukchansi Yokuts

AT first there was no fire. The turtle had it all. He sat on it and covered it up. He lived far up in the east in the mountains. Coyote went to that place. He lay down like a piece of wood. The people who lived there came by and saw him. "I am going to take this piece of wood," they said. They took him home and put him in the fire. Coyote tried to get into the fire under the turtle. The turtle said'. "Stop pushing me." Now Coyote got some of the fire. Then he ran down-hill with it westward into this country, where then there was no fire and it was cold. He caught a quail and with its fat he made his fire blaze up. Now the people first all became warm. The Mono (Shoshoneans) were far back up in the hills; the Chukchansi (Yokuts) in the middle; the Pohonichi (Miwok) were the ones who received the fire. Coyote was one of them. That is why the Mono cannot speak well; it is too cold where they live.

Coyote made the eagle the chief of the people. They enjoyed themselves and made dances. They were warm now because they had fire. They lived well. They wore no clothes. Some men wore a blanket of rabbit skins or of deer skin; others wore nothing. They used hollow stones to cook in, made of soft red stone. The eagle told them: "Go out and catch rabbits," and then they caught rabbits to eat. To get salt they went beyond the North Fork of the San Joaquin.

POHONICHI MIWOK. THE ORIGIN OF DEATH

Told among the Chukchansi Yokuts

WHEN the first person died Coyote was south of him, the meadow-lark to the north. Now the dead person began to stink. The meadow-lark smelled it. He did not like it. Coyote said: "I think I will make him get up. The meadow-lark said: "No, do not. There will be too many. They will become so many that they will eat each other." Coyote said: "That is nothing. I do not like people to die." But the meadow-lark told him: "No, it is not well to have too many. There will be others instead of those that die. A man will have many children. The old people will die but the young will live." Then Coyote said nothing more. So from that time on people have always died. Coyote said: "It will be best to put them into the fire." And so the dead were burned.

POHONICHI MIWOK. THE BEAR AND DEER CHILDREN

Told among the Chukchansi Yokuts

THE thunders were two boys with supernatural powers. Their mother was the deer. The grizzly bear also had two children. The two women went to the creek looking for clover (Chukchansi: malich). Now they loused each other. Then the bear bit the back of the deer's neck and killed her. The two deer-children made a little sweat-house. After the bear had killed and eaten their mother, they killed the two bear-children in this sweathouse with fire. Then they struck the ground and made a noise and fled to their grandfather. He was powerful and had a large sweat-house. The bear pursued them. She had nearly caught them when they escaped into the sweat house. The bear put in her head looking for them. Her hind legs were still outside. The boys' grandfather had supernatural powers with fire; his amulet was a white rock at the top of the house. When all the bear's body except her hind legs was in the house as she looked about for the two boys, the white fire-rock entered her anus and burned her to death inside. Then the two young deer became thunders. After awhile they also had supernatural powers. They made so much noise in the house that their grandfather was afraid. They went up above, where they still are.[27]

The half-Chukchansi from whom the Pohonichi tales just given were obtained did not seem to know any story of the stealing of the sun, of a hero who is dug out of the ground as a child, and of a contest between the coyote and the lizard determining the shape of the human hand.

GASHOWU YOKUTS. THE BEGINNING OF THE WORLD

THE prairie falcon and the raven made the earth at a time when everything was water. The beaver, the otter, the mud-hen, the mallard duck, and a duck called potikh dived and tried to reach bottom, but could not do so. Then k'uik'ui, a small duck, dived, reached the bottom, and grasped the sand there. As he rose up, it washed out of his hands, his mouth, and his ears. Only a little was left under his finger-nail. When he came to the surface, he gave this to the prairie falcon. The prairie falcon had tobacco. This he mixed with the sand. Then he divided it, and gave half to the raven, whom he called his friend. They went far to the north. There they separated. The prairie falcon sent the raven to go southward on the west. He himself came southward along the east where these mountains are now. As they went they dropped the sand from between the thumb and finger. As the sand fell into the water it began to boil and the world grew from underneath. Then the raven surpassed the prairie falcon. These large mountains which are now here were then in the west. When the prairie falcon arrived he saw that the raven's mountains were the larger. Then he changed them about. He put one in the place of the other without the raven's knowledge.

So if it had not been for k'uik'ui and the prairie falcon the world would not have been made. But it was the prairie falcon who first wanted the world.

GASHOWU YOKUTS. THE ORIGIN OF DEATH

A person was dying. Then some people said: "Let it be that he lies outside for three days. Then he will get up and be a person again." Now there was one newly married man, the meadow-lark. He did not like the dead person lying near his house because the body smelled. He said: "We will take the dead one away and burn him." So the people were persuaded. They built a pile of wood, laid the body on it, and burned it. Thus the people of old times did, and so people die now and do not come back.

GASHOWU YOKUTS. THE OWL DOCTOR

THE prairie falcon made war on the northerners and was killed. Coyote claimed to be a medicine man and was the first to doctor him. He was merely a pretender who wanted to obtain pay. Then others, all owls, doctored him. Hihina, the large owl, sodut, the white owl, wedjiji, the ground owl, and hihimcha, the small owl, were the ones who doctored him. It was the white owl that cured him.

GASHOWU YOKUTS. COYOTE, THE HAWK, AND THE CONDOR

THERE was a woman whom no one was able to marry, except finally Coyote. He overcame her. She was wachwach, a handsome species of hawk. She lived alone. The wolf and Coyote and their families lived in one place with other people. Many men went out to hunt deer but never found any. The wildcat and the weasel and others went. The magpie was "beniti." He could see from inside his house and know everything. He saw that the hawk-woman had supernatural power. She was able to kill a deer and immediately eat it entirely, leaving only the skin. Then the wolf and Coyote found the woman. She gave them an abundance of acorn mush. She also cooked dried deer meat for them and gave it to them to take home. She said to them: "Tell no one, but when you want more for your children, come and get it." The wolf and Coyote arrived at night. Their poor little children had to eat the meat they brought slowly, so that no one would hear them. Nevertheless the magpie knew it. Then the people also could smell the meat. Knowing that the two brothers had meat, they watched at night. Then they saw them return and the old woman get up, take the meat. cook it, and all of them eat. Then the watchers reported to the others: "They are killing deer but give none of the meat away." The eagle was the chief. The dove was his messenger (winatum). Thinking he would ask advice of the magpie, the eagle sent the dove to him. The magpie only laughed at the messenger. "Yes, Coyote and the wolf have found a supernatural woman. She lives beyond this hill. She has more dried meat than she can use. She keeps the deer inside the hill under ground. That is where she gets the meat." Then all the people went to that place, to the woman, so that it became necessary for her to give them meat. When Coyote and the wolf arrived there in the evening, they found all the people there already. The weasel, the hawk called wakhwukh, and others had dressed themselves finely in order to marry her, but she would not have it. Finally all of them said: "Let us go home." They went, but Coyote lay there, apparently sick with fever and chills, and unable to walk. The woman said: "You go too." Coyote told her: "I am sick. I cannot. Perhaps later on I will be able." Then the woman made a fire inside the house. Coyote thought how he might enter it. He, too, had supernatural power. Then he wanted the wind to blow the house to pieces. He said: "Pu!" and a wind storm came. It began to tear the thatching from the house. The woman ran about trying to mend it but could not. Then Coyote said: "Give me the binding and I will tie it." She did not like to touch him, but to save her house she handed it to him. Now it was dark and rained. Coyote said: "I cannot sleep here. Let me sleep inside in the corner by the door." But she would not let him. He said: "I will die. If you wish me to freeze to death let me lie here." Then she allowed him to come in, and he lay near the door, shivering. She knew what he wanted. He was thinking: "I want to sleep with her." Then she said: "No, you cannot. You are no good." Coyote laughed. "How does she know what I think?" he thought. "I heard it," she said. Coyote lay there and looked over towards her. "What do you want now?" she asked. Then Coyote began to think of sexual intercourse with her. She did not like that. She was stronger than he and overcame him. He could not do anything to her. He went to sleep where he lay. Then at last the woman began to think of him. At once Coyote knew it in his sleep. He woke up and said: "You want mine! I have a good one!" She too was desirous now and let him lie with her. But though she allowed him to embrace her she would not let him come nearer. She wanted once more to try to overcome him. She went out as if to urinate, took a rattles snake, put it into herself, and returned. Then she spread herself and invited him. He knew what she had done. Also going out to urinate, he by his supernatural power obtained a stick of hard wood (takha) from the cast. Putting it on himself, he returned to the woman. He approached the stick, the rattlesnake bit it, lost its teeth, and was harmless. Coyote said: "Ah! Now throw yours away and I will throw mine." She did so and he married her.

Coyote had one son from this woman, wech, the condor, who was to become a great gambler. At night they put the baby into water. After three days he could walk. Soon he was able to gamble. Then he was a man. Coyote was rich, constantly making beads from bone and other materials, and encouraged his son to gamble. Then the boy went north. Then he saw a large owl, hihina, and wishing to kill him, aimed at him. The owl, who was a doctor, was angry and flew up into a hollow tree. There he began to sing:

Hu hu hu [1] witcailac [2] min [3] put-onun [4]

Hu hu hu [1], condor becomes [2] your [3] son [4].

As he sang this, the young man who had been so handsome began to have feathers all over his body. His female relatives who were with him tried to hold him, but they could not, and he turned into a condor. They said to Coyote: "Kill the owl before he changes him completely!" But Coyote only cried and did nothing. Now the young man Was entirely a condor. He shook himself, rose, and flew off. The women followed, but he flew away from them. Coyote returned. His wife knew what had happened. Then she took a rattlesnake once more. This time he did not know it, was bitten, and died.

Now the condor lived above and came down to earth to kill people for food. He thought of his mother, went to her, and brought her up with him. He tried to make her, too, eat people, but she would not do so. He brought two little boys and a little girl. These he kept as pets. He called them his dogs. As he was about to go off again he told his mother: "Feed them well. When I return I will eat them." When he was gone the woman said to the children: "He will kill us all. He has nearly exterminated the people now. When he has finished them he will go hither up in the sky. Then he will come down and eat us. When he comes back you must shoot him." She gave the two boys bows and arrows. Then the condor came back from the earth below and went to drink. He drank half a day. The two boys shot at him, one from each side. For half a day they shot as fast as they could, beginning as soon as he started to drink. The little girl kept dragging the arrows back to them and they shot them again and again. The condor never gave notice, but continued to drink. Now the half day was nearly over. The woman had made a hole. She put the children in, went in herself, and covered the hole. Then the condor stopped drinking. Now he began to feel something. Leaving the dead bodies he had brought with him, he started upward. His mother said: "If he flies straight, he will reach the place above, and it will be the end of us. But if he flies to the side and zigzags and falls, he will be killed." He flew straight up. He was already nearly out of sight. Then suddenly he shot to one side, zigzagged, dropped, struck, and was dead. They burned him. Then his eyes burst and flew out and were lost in the brush. If they had been able to find the eyes and put them back in the fire there would have been no condors in the world.

Then the woman and the little girl went down from the sky on a rope of down feathers, going through the hole in the sky through which the condor used to pass. The two boys went southward in the sky until they came to where the sky and the earth meet. There they descended to the earth. Then they came to people without mouths, who neither talked nor ate. They killed deer, roasted them, smelled of the meat, and threw it out-doors. In the same way they only smelled of their acorn mush. The two boys came to them, entered the house, took hold of the meat that was cooking, and began to eat. The people there made a protesting gesture, meaning. "Do not. It will come out from you," again indicating by a gesture. Neverthless {sic} the boys ate. Then they asked the chief: "Have you a tongue inside?" He shook his head. "Have you teeth?" Again he shook his head. Then they offered to try to cut open a mouth for one of them so that he would be like themselves and could eat. It was agreed and the two boys took obsidian and cut a mouth for one of those people. Soon the man could eat and talk. Then he said:

T-ipînii [1] panîii [2] tcicîii [3] nah'èii [4] lukînii [5] bidîkii [6].

Supernatural-ones [1] arrived [2], cut [3], ate [4], belly filled [5], defecated [6],

He spoke thus because he could not talk yet correctly. If he had spoken right he would have said:

T-ipni panac tcicîni nah'ac lokònoc

Then this man cut mouths for others, and they cut still others, mid so they did to each otheruntil all could eat and talk. The two boys returned home.

TRUHOHI YOKUTS. THE BEGINNING OF THE WORLD

Told by a Tachi Yokuts

FAR in the south was a mountain. It was the only land. Everything else was water. The eagle was the chief. The people had nothing to eat. They were eating the earth and it was nearly gone. Then Coyote said: "Can we not obtain earth? Can we not make mountains?" The eagle said: "I do not know how."

Coyote said: "There is a man that we will ask." Then they got the magpie. The eagle said: "Can we obtain earth?" The magpie said: "Yes." "Where?" "Right below us." Then all the ducks dived and tried to bring up the earth. Some were gone half a day. They could not reach the bottom and died and floated up. The eagle said: "When you reach the ground take hold of it and bite it, and fill your nose and ears." For six days they dived and found nothing. There was only one more to go down, the mudhen. Then the eagle said: "Now you go. Let us see if you can find the earth." The mudhen said: "Good." Then it dived. It was gone for a day and a night. In the morning it came up. It was dead. They looked it over. It had earth in its nails, its cars, and its nose. Then they made the earth from this ground. They mixed it with chiyu seeds and from this they made the earth. After six days the eagle said to the wolf: "Now go around." Then the wolf went where the Sierra Nevada now is and around to the west and came back along where the Coast Range is. The eagle said: "Do not touch it for six days. Let it dry first." All the people said: "Very well, we will let it become dry." But soon

Coyote said: "I will try it. It is getting hard now." He traveled along where the Sierras are. That is why these are rough and broken now. It is from his running over the soft earth. Then he turned west and went back along the Coast Range. That is why there are mountains there also. Coyote made it so. Now the eagle sent out the prairie falcon and the raven (Khotoi). He told them: "Go around the world and see if the earth is hard yet." Then the prairie falcon went north along the Sierra Nevada and Khotoi went north along the Coast Range. Each came back the way he had gone. Now at first the Sierra Nevada was not so high as the Coast Range. When the two returned the eagle said: "How is the earth? Is it hard?" "Yes," they said. Then the prairie falcon said "Look at my mountains. They are the highest," but Khotoi said: "No, mine are higher." The prairie falcon said: "No, your, do not amount to anything. They are low." Then the eagle and Coyote sent the people to different places. They said: "You go to that place with your people. You go to that spring." So they sent them off, and the people went to the different places where they are now. They were still animals, but they became people. For a little while after they had all gone the eagle and Coyote stayed there. Then Coyote said: "Where will you go?" The eagle said: "I am thinking about it. I think I will go up." Coyote said: "Where shall I live?" The eagle said: "Here." But Coyote said: "No, I will go with you." The eagle told him: "No, you must stay here. You will have to look after this place here." So they talked for six days. Then the eagle took all his things. "Goodby," he said, "I am going." Then he went. Coyote looked up. He said: "I am going too." "You have no wings. You cannot," said the eagle. "I will go," said Coyote, and he went. Now they are together in the sky above.

TRUHOHI YOKUTS. THE THEFT OF FIRE

Told by a Tachi Yokuts

THERE was no fire. It was very cold. Then the eagle told the roadrunner and the fox to go out. These two were good runners. Coyote said: "Let the crow go. He is good at looking about." The eagle said: "They are better;" but he let the crow go. Then Coyote said: "I am going too," though the eagle wanted him to stay. Then the eagle told the crow: "Start early. If you see fire anywhere tell us." Late in the day the crow saw fire in the west. He came back and said: "They have fire there." Then the eagle sent out the roadrunner and the fox. Coyote and the crow went with them. They went directly north along the Coast Range. Before, when the crow had gone alone, he first went eastward and then north and then to the west and back south. Now Coyote said: "Wait until the sun is down. Then we will steal it. They agreed. Now it was dark in the west. Then Coyote said: "Now they are all asleep." The crow said: "We will not all go there. Let one who can jump well take the fire. You, fox, go." Coyote said: "I will go too. I am a good jumper too." The crow said: "No, we will be killed." But Coyote said: "No, we are all good runners. And I will take the fire. Even if you come with me it is I who will take the fire." Then they came to one end of the village. "Here is good fire," they said. They took fire, and put it in a net-sack. Then Coyote told them: "Run ahead. I am going to kill this little one." "No, do not," said the fox. "Yes, I will," said Coyote. Then the fox and the others went ahead. Coyote took the child, threw it in the fire, and killed it. Then he leaped out of the house and ran. It was another coyote who was living there. He called out: "Take care! Someone has come!"

Now as the fire-stealers ran, their path was the San Joaquin river. The fog (?), gumun, and a duck, wolwul, pursued them. Coyote jumped from side to side and the pursuers ran here and there after him. That is why the river is crooked. They kept on running southward. Then Coyote reached his sweat-house. He entered and closed it. They could not catch him. He had the fire inside. He had succeeded in taking it away from them. Then in the morning they made fire there. From that day they had fire and were well off.

TRUHOHI YOKUTS. THE ORIGIN OF DEATH

Told by a Tachi Yokuts

THERE were two insects, Shoyo and Kokwiteit.[28] The latter was a chief. He, did not want many people to live. He gathered the people and said: "We will go. I do not know where. We must go somewhere. It will fill up. It is best if we make it that medicine-men will kill people. Then there will be a great ceremony for the dead." Coyote liked that. The others did not like it. Coyote said: "When a chief or one of his family dies we will go to his village. We will have a great gathering. We will dance and enjoy ourselves." Then the people liked the idea. But it was Kokwiteit who was the cause. So now, here in this world, if one meets a kokwiteit in the road, people say: "There will be too many; let us kill him." So they kill him. Shoyo did not want people to die, but Kokwiteit made it that they do.

TACHI YOKUTS. THE OWNERS OF THE SUN

IN the Tachi territory in the Coast Range is a circle of large rocks. These are certain people who had the sun. They kept it in the middle of the circle, just above their heads. Coyote and the eagle took it away from them. Then they became ashamed and turned to stone. If one speaks to them now, they still answer; but it is hard to reach that place, for they do not like to be seen by anyone, and when one approaches it he meets wind and rain.

TACHI YOKUTS. THE RACE OF THE ANTELOPE AND DEER

THE antelope and the deer were together. The antelope said: "I can beat you running." The deer said: "I think not." The antelope said: "Well, let us try." The deer said: "We shall run for six days," and the antelope agreed. The deer said: "Let us go south and run northward." Then they went far to the south "across the ocean" (or Tulare Lake), in order to run northward to the end of the world. The antelope said: "This will be my path on the west here. You take the path on the east." The deer agreed. Then they started. Their path was the milky way. On the side where the antelope ran there is a wide path; on the other side there are patches. That is where the deer jumped. The antelope had said: "If I win, all this will be my country and you will have to bide in the brush." The deer said: "Very well, and if I win it will be the same for me." Then they ran and the antelope won. So now he has the plains to live in, but the deer hides in the brush.

TACHI YOKUTS. THE PLEIADES

THE Pleiades were five girls and a flea, baakil. The girls sang and played all night in the sky. The flea constantly went with them. They did not like the other men that came to them; they liked only him. They did not like the other men that came to them ran away, but the flea went with them. And they let him marry them. He married all five. Now he turned into a flea, and in summer became sick with the itch. The girls did not like him any longer. They said: "Let us run away. Where shall we go?" Then they agreed to go east together. "When shall we go?" they said. "As soon as he sleeps." Now the flea slept and the five got up and went off. After they were far away the flea woke up and thought: "Where are my wives?" He found that they had gone away.

He thought: "Where shall I go?" He went east. At last he came in sight of them, just before he reached the ocean. He said: "I will catch you." They said: "He is coming. Let us go on." They ran on again. Then one asked: "Do you see him again!" Another said: "Yes, he is near." Then they said: "Let us go up into the air. Then he cannot come with us." Then they went up. But the man rose, too. That is why there are five stars close together now in the Pleiades and one at the side. That one is he, the flea.[29]

TACHI YOKUTS. THE WOLF AND THE CRANE

THE wolf constantly hunted, but never gave his wife and two boys any meat. Once in the morning He went hunting. Then his wife, the crane, ran off. He returned and found her gone. He followed her. He was angry and wanted to kill her. He saw her and tried to shoot her, but she was high up in the air. Slowly she settled and at last lit far off. Then he shot and hit her. He went to her. With her bill she tried to stab him. He used an arrow to ward off her blows, and tried to stab her. Then she pierced his breast and knocked him down. She stabbed him again and again, until she killed him. Then she went off with her boys. They turned into stars in the sky. She is in advance; her two boys are following her. They are called yibish, the three stars of Orion.

TACHI YOKUTS. THE BALD EAGLE AND THE PRAIRIE FALCON

AT a mountain southwest from the north end of Tulare Lake the ground is red and white. There the bald eagle, owik, lived. He used to take away men's wives. If they became angry he killed them. The prairie falcon, limik, lived farther north in the Coast Range with the Tachi. The eagle took away his wife. Then the prairie falcon pursued him. He fought him. He broke his head with a rock and killed him. The bald eagle's brains and blood turned the ground white and red.

TACHI YOKUTS. THE THUNDER TWINS

ALL the land in the plains north of Tulare Lake where the Tachi lived in summer was burned bare. Nothing was growing there, no seeds and no tule. The people were starving. In the mountains to the west, where the Tachi lived in winter, there were two little boys, twins. They were covered with sores and stank. Whenever they had finished eating, their father whipped them out of the house. They came back crying, but their parents took no pity on them. Only their grandmother took care of them Now the chief of the people in the plains said to his people: "Go about the land and see if you cannot find food. We will move wherever anything is growing." Then runners went southwestward. There they found a high mountain and near it a little lake, which is now dry. There were tule roots and seeds to be had there and the people moved there. Now the father and mother of the two boys abandoned them. But their grandmother stayed with them and cried over them. For two years they lived in this way. Sometimes the old woman found a few tule roots, and with these she fed the boys and they grew. Now, when they were two years older, they no longer wanted to eat anything. They turned into thunders. At a high mountain west of the north end of the lake is a spring. There the boys went and there they are living now. They told their grandmother: "Grandmother, next month we shall have many fish from that water." Then in a month the spring was full of fish. They caught them and dried them. The boys did not eat any of them, for they had turned into supernatural beings. Now their mother's brother, who had gone away with their parents, came back, bringing the boys a little food. Then they shot him. They nearly killed him, but cured him again. He told them:

"When your father and your mother come, kill them." Then he went back with the fish which they had given him. When he returned, he told the people: "They are well off now. They have much to eat." Then the boys' father and mother went there with other people. The boys shot at them and killed their parents and those that went with them. Next day those of the people who had not yet gone, said: "Perhaps they were given many fish and that is why they did not come back last night." But their mother's brother told them why they should not go to that place. So the remainder of the people stayed where they were and were not killed. The mountain where the thunder twins live is called chenhali.

TACHI YOKUTS. THE VISIT TO THE DEAD

A Tachi had a fine wife who died and was buried. Her husband went to her grave and dug a hole near it. There he stayed watching, not eating, not using only tobacco. After two nights he saw that she came up, brushed the earth off herself, and started to go to the island of the dead. The man tried to seize her but could not hold her. She went southeast and he followed her. Whenever he tried to hold her she escaped. He kept trying to seize her, however, and delayed her. At daybreak she stopped. He stayed there, but could not see her. When it began to be dark the woman got up again and went on. She turned westward and crossed Tulare Lake (or its inlet). At daybreak the man again tried to seize her but could not hold her. She stayed in that place during the day. The man remained in the same place, but again he could not see her. There was a good trail there, and he could see the footprints of his dead friends and relatives. In the evening his wife got up again and went on. They came to a river which flows westward toward San Luis Obispo, the river of the Tulamni (the description fits the Santa Maria, but the Tulamni are in the Tulare drainage, on and about Buena Vista lake). There the man caught up with his wife and there they stayed all day. He still had had nothing to eat. In the evening she went on again, now northward. Then somewhere to the west of the Tachi country he caught up with her once more and they spent the day there. In the evening the woman got up and they went on northward, across the San Joaquin river, to the north or east of it. Again he overtook his wife. Then she said: "What are you going to do? I am nothing now. How can you get my body back? Do you think you shall be able to do it?" He said: "I think so." She said: "I think not. I am going to a different kind of a place now." From daybreak on that man stayed there. In the evening the woman started once more and went down along the river, but he overtook her again. She did not talk to him. Then they stayed all day, and at night went on again. Now they were close to the island of the dead. It was joined to the land by a rising and falling bridge called ch'eleli. Under this bridge a river ran swiftly. The dead passed over this. When they were on the bridge, a bird suddenly fluttered up beside them and frightened them. Many fell off into the river, where they turned into fish. Now the chief of the dead said: "Somebody has come." They told him: "There are two. One of them is alive; he stinks." The chief said: "Do not let him cross." When the woman came on the island, he asked her: "You have a companion?" and she told him: "Yes, my husband." He asked her: "Is he coming here?" She said: "I do not know. He is alive." They asked the man: "Do you want to come to this country?" He said: "Yes." Then they told him: "Wait. I will see the chief." They told the chief: "He says that he wants to come to this country. We think he does not tell the truth." "Well, let him come across." Now they intended to frighten him off the bridge. They said: "Come on. The chief says you can cross." Then the bird (kacha) flew up and tried to scare him, but did not make him fall off the bridge into the water. So they brought him before the chief. The chief said: "This is a bad country. You should not have come. We have only your wife's soul (ilit). She has left her bones with her body. I do not think we can give her back to you." In the evening they danced. It was a round dance and they shouted. The chief said to the man: "Look at your wife in the middle of the crowd. To-morrow you will see no one." Now the man stayed there three days. Then the chief said to some of the people: "Bring that woman. her husband wants to talk to her." They brought the woman to him. He asked her: "Is this your husband?" She said: "Yes." He asked her: "Do you think you will go back to him?" She said: "I do not think so. What do you wish?" The chief said: "I think not. You must stay here. You cannot go back. You are worthless now." Then He said to the man: "Do you want to sleep with your wife?" He said: "Yes, for a while. I want to sleep with her and talk with her." Then he was allowed to sleep with her that night and they talked together. At daybreak the woman was vanished and he was sleeping next to a fallen oak. The chief said to him: "Get up. It is late." He opened his eyes and saw an oak instead of his wife. The chief said: "You see that we cannot make your wife as she was. She is no good now. It is best that you go back. You have a good country there." But the man said: "No, I will stay." The chief told him: "No, do not. Come back here whenever you like, but go back now." Nevertheless the man stayed there six days. Then he said: "I am going back." Then in the morning he started to go home. The chief told him: "When you arrive, hide yourself. Then after six days emerge and make a dance." Now the man returned. He told his parents: "Make me a small house. In six days I will come out and dance." Now he stayed there five days. Then his friends began to know that he had come back. "Our relative has come back," they all said. Now the man was in too much of a hurry. After five days he came out. In the evening he began to dance and danced all night, telling what he saw. In the morning, when he had stopped dancing, he went to bathe. Then a rattlesnake bit him. He died. So he went back to the island. He is there now. It is through him that the people know how it is there. Every two days the island becomes full. Then the chief gathers the people. "You must swim," he says. The people stop dancing and bathe. Then the bird frightens them, and some turn to fish, and some to ducks; only a few come out of the water again as people. In this way room is made when the island is too full. The name of the chief there is Kandjidji.

WÜKCHAMNI YOKUTS. THE BEGINNING OF THE WORLD

Told by a Yaudanchi Yokuts

EVERYTHING was water except a very small piece of ground. On this were the eagle and Coyote. Then the turtle swam to them. They sent it to dive for the earth at the bottom of the water. The turtle barely succeeded in reaching the bottom and touching it with its foot. When it came up again, all the earth seemed washed out. Coyote looked closely at its nails. At last he found a grain of earth. Then he and the eagle took this and laid it down. From it they made the earth as large as it is. From the earth they also made six men and six women. They sent these out in pairs in different directions and the people separated. After a time the eagle sent the Coyote to see what the people were doing. Coyote came back and said: "They are doing something bad. They are eating the earth. One side is already gone." The eagle said: "That is bad. Let us make something for them to eat. Let us send the dove to find something." The dove went out. It found a single grain of meal. The eagle and Coyote put this down on the ground. Then the earth became covered with seeds and fruit. Now they told the people to eat these. When the seeds were dry and ripe the people gathered them. Then the people increased and spread all over. But the water is still under the world.

YAUDANCHI YOKUTS. THE ORIGIN OF FIRE

THE people in the foothills had no fire. Only to the west in the plains was there a man who had fire, and he had it all. Now when he slept, the antelope, selected for its swiftness, was sent to steal his fire. It took it and fled. It was again in sight of the place from which it had started, when a rain came, which put out the fire. Then others tried to bring it. The last was the jackrabbit. After he had stolen the fire, he bid in a thick brush, shek'ei. There he burrowed. Then he crouched over the fire, holding it in his hands under his belly. From this the palms of his hands are black. When he stole the fire it was not extinguished; and so he obtained it for the people.

YAUDANCHI YOKUTS. THE EAGLE AND THE CONDOR

THE eagle was chief. The condor did not like him. He tried to supersede him as chief. Flying high in the air, he saw a bloody deer on the ground. "Now I will have something to eat," bethought. He lit and began to peck at the deer. The eagle, hidden under the brush on which the deer was lying, caught him by the foot. "Now I have you! I will kill you," he said. The condor said: "Let me go. You can be chief again. I will go away." Then the eagle released him and was chief once more.

YAUDANCHI YOKUTS. THE EAGLE'S SON

THE eagle had a boy. He said to him: "Do not go over that hill." The boy grew up. One day, saying: "I am just going off somewhere," he went over the hill. When he came back he said to his grandmother: "I saw something on the other side of that hill." "What did you see?" she asked. "Many people," he said. Next day he went over again. Then a number of girls who were gathering clover saw him. They were the woodpecker, the bluejay, the quail, the mountain quail, and the rat. When he came near them they spat on him the clover they were eating and ran off. The boy went toward the house in that place. Coyote who was there prepared to shoot him. Moving his band over his mouth he shouted: "Wuwuwuwuwuwu! Some one is coming." The boy was carrying arrows also, but did not take them out of his quiver. Coyote came near him, drew his bow, and shot. He missed the boy. Then the dog, the right side of whose face was black, shot. He missed also. When the two saw that they could not hit the boy, they said to him: "Come, my friend, sit here." Then he came and sat down with them. When he said: "I must go," Coyote told him: "Well, come again." The boy returned home. He told his father: "I have been to see people over the hill. I want to go again to-morrow." Then the eagle said: "Do not go. You will be killed." The boy told him: "They have already tried to kill me." Next day he went again. He came to the same place and the girls were there as before. He was dressed beautifully now. He looked so fine that the girls did not know him again. This time they tried to embrace him. They were so jealous that they were ready to fight one another. They all went to where he lived. All of them had long hair and were beautiful; and each came carrying a load of food. The bluejay went into the house and said to the boy's grandmother: "Go outside and get my load., I have brought something to eat. I want to live with this young man." The old woman did not bring it in. All the girls came in, one after another, and each told the old woman to take her food inside, but she did not do it. Then the woodpecker came in. She was the only one of them who had not spit on the boy when he first came to them. When she said to the old woman: "Bring in my load. I want to live here," the old woman said: "Yes," and carried it in. Then the other girls were angry, and struck the woodpecker on the head, and the blood that came is the red that is now on the woodpecker's head. Then the woodpecker threw ashes on the bluejay, and made her blue, She threw fire on the mountain quail, which therefore is spotted with red. She rubbed charcoal on the quail, from which its head is black, and she threw fire on the rat, from which this has a reddish belly. Then the woodpecker lived there. After a time the young man went over the hill again. He went to fight Coyote and the black-faced dog. He shot both and killed them. Then the eagle said to him: "Let us go and kill all of them." Then those people all fled and scattered over the country.

YAUDANCHI YOKUTS. THE PRAIRIE FALCON FIGHTS[30]

LONG ago the prairie falcon (limik) lived alone. He came to a village. He returned. Then he went again. He reached a rock. He sat on top of it and laid his bow down on it. Then he thought: "It will be good if I kill them." He started again. Then he began the fight. He shot at them. At once the people there all became angry. There was a great battle. He killed them all. Then he hung up the hair of the killed on trees. It can be seen still (as moss) at a place called khodomo (probably in the territory of the Shoshonean Tübatulabal or Pitanisha).

YAUDANCHI YOKUTS. THE PRAIRIE FALCON'S WIFE[31]

THE prairie falcon lived there. His wife, the duck, lived there. Coyote lived there with them. The three were there. Then the prairie falcon went off. He told Coyote: "Do not sleep." Then the prairie falcon's wife went off from there. She gathered seeds. Then they [the woman and Coyote] returned. The prairie falcon also returned. They all returned safely. Then in the morning the prairie falcon again went. He told Coyote: "Do not sleep." Then the prairie falcon's swife again went. Now Coyote slept while she gathered seeds. Then the condor saw her from above. Then he came from there. He lit near the prairie falcon's wife. He said to her: "We will go up." The woman said to him: "I will not go." He said to her: "We will go." Then she agreed. She said to him: "How shall I go?" He said to her: "Lie down right here on my back." Then they two went off. They went up. Then they arrived there, far off, at the hole of our world. An old man was there. Now the two lived there. The woman was with him. The old man there guarded the woman. Then the prairie falcon came home. He said: "Where is my wife?" Then he [Coyote] said: "I do not know." He said to him: "What did you do? Did you sleep?" He said: "Yes, I slept." Now they two looked for her. They did not find her. Then they sent the dove to look. The dove did not find her. Then they sent the buzzard also. The buzzard did not find her. They sent also the large fly, and he did not find her. Then they sent the large lizard, k'ondjedja (species?). Then the lizard came out from the rock. He looked about. He saw the hole of our world above. Then the lizard said: "Far up." Then they sent the large fly again. He went up. He came there above to the hole of our world. Then the fly saw that woman. From there he went back. He came to the prairie falcon. He told the prairie falcon: "Your wife is above there." Now the condor went. He said to the old man: "Do not say this to my wife; do not tell her: 'Bring water!' Well, now I am going." Then the condor went. Now the prairie falcon arrived there where the water was. Then the prairie falcon saw his wife there. He told his wife: "Do not say anything." Then he went from there. He arrived there. Then the old man said to him: "Where are you going?" Then he said: "I am traveling for nothing." Then he said: "I am going now." He told his wife: "Come to me there where the water is." Then his wife said: "Yes." Then the prairie falcon had gone. That old man slept. Then the prairie falcon's wife went. Then the prairie falcon's wife came to him at the water. Then they went. Now they two arrived at their house.

YAUDANCHI YOKUTS. THE PRAIRIE FALCON LOSES[32]

THE prairie falcon shouted because he beat all the people at playing. Then the dove and the meadow-lark told Coyote: "Go and cuckold him." Coyote said: "Yes, I will do it." He went up the mountain. Halfway up was a spring. From there Coyote went to the summit. He rolled himself down. At each bound he cried: "I am the prairie falcon, I am the prairie falcon!" When he had rolled to the spring he looked at himself in the water. He resembled the prairie falcon a little. He went to the top of the mountain again and rolled down once more, crying: "I am the prairie falcon." Then he looked at himself in the spring and thought: "I am a little more like him." Again he went to the top and rolled down. Then he looked at himself in the water. Now he was the prairie falcon. Then he said: "Let me have a stick." Then he had his stick and went to the prairie falcon's house. He leaned the stick against the entrance and said to the woman: "Give me my ball." She asked him: "Where is it?" "It is there at our pillow. She could not find it. So she said: "Come, get it yourself." Coyote entered the house, lifted up the pillow, and there was the ball. The prairie falcon's wife asked: "Why did you not take it when you went?" Then he hugged her. And then he cohabited with her. When he went out of the house, the woman saw his tail sticking out. He went where they were playing. Now the dove won and the meadow-lark won, and the prairie falcon lost. He lost all his beads.

YAUDANCHI YOKUTS. WAR OF THE FOO-THILL AND PLAINS PEOPLE

THE birds and animals from the mountains (foothills) went to war with the animals of the lake below. With the party from the mountains was Coyote. He had a large quiver full of arrows. In the morning he got up, knotted his hair behind, took his bow, and called to all, "Get up, get up, or I will kill you. I am ready to go to war." Now they started. All the way down into the plains Coyote led the way and hurried the others. Alongside him was the humming-bird. They two were the leaders. There were three owls, (? tuwidech) with the party. One of these carried an inexhaustible supply of arrow point; in his mouth; another carried sinew; and a third feathers for arrow-shafts. As the arrows became used during the fight, they produced these materials and kept the people supplied. So they fought. The people from the mountains beat those of the plains. But there were two that they could not kill, the fish epis and the turtle. One of these was slippery, the other was hard, and the arrows glanced off their backs. Then Coyote broke his leg, took out the bone, stuck it into the end of his arrow, and shot. He struck the fish in the back of its neck and killed it. Then he shot at the turtle and struck it in its head aperture and killed it.

Now the eagle, who was the chief of all, sent off the victorious mountain people. He said: "You cannot live here any longer. You must go away. Where do you want to go?" Coyote said: "Wishawishawisha! Wishawishawisha! Wishawishawisha! I do not want to go." The humming-bird agreed with him. The eagle, said: "Well, what are you going to become? What will you be? I am going to fly high up in the air and live on squirrels and sometimes on deer." The dog said: "I will stay with people and be their friend. I will follow them, and perhaps I will get something to eat in that way." The buzzard said: "When something dies I will smell it. I will go there and eat it." The crow said: "When I see something lying dead I will pick its eyes." Coyote said: "I will go about killing grasshoppers. That is how I will live." The humming-bird said: "I will go to the flowers and get my food from them." The condor said: "I will not stay here. I will go far off into the mountains. Perhaps I will, find something there." The woodpecker said: "I will get acorns and make holes in the trees." The bluejay said: "I am going to make trees grow over the hills. I will work." The rat said: "I will go where there are old trees and make my house in them." The mouse said: "I will run here and there and everywhere. I shall have holes and perhaps I can live in that way." The trout said: "I will live in the water and perhaps I can find something to eat there."

That was the time they stopped being like us and scattered.

YAUDANCHI YOKUTS. THUNDER AND WHIRLWIND

THUNDER and Whirlwind each had a boy. Thunder said: "You cannot find your boy. I have hidden him from you." He had put him away enclosed in stone. Then the Whirlwind rushed. He whirled by the rock, tore the top off, and found his boy. Then the Whirlwind took Thunder's boy and whirled off with him. He took him far away into the water. Thunder began to look for his son. It became foggy. There was fine rain all around. Thunder came with great noise. He hurled the rain and fog aside. He found his son. So each of them succeeded in getting his boy again.

YAUDANCHI YOKUTS. MIKITI[33]

Learned by the informant from a Yauelmani Yokuts

MITIKI lived with her daughter at Chit'at (clover). They were there alone, she and her daughter. It was spring and the clover grew. Then her daughter went out to gather clover. Mikiti told her: "Do not go far." Then for a long time she did not go far. After awhile she began to go farther. Then she saw good clover mid gathered it mid brought it home. Then Mikiti ate it. "Where did you get the good clover?" she asked. Her daughter said: "I went farther away." Then Mikiti said: "Do not go there again." The next day the girl went again. She came where it was brushy. "Do not taste the clover when you gather it," Mikiti had told her. Now when she was in the brushy place she found good clover. She gathered a great deal. She put it all into her carrying net. When she had done this she saw a bunch of clover. She thought: "It looks very fine." Then she ate it. She had not yet swallowed it when a grizzly bear came out of the brush. He ate her up entirely. Now this girl had been with child. When she did not come back to the house Mikiti said: "I knew it. You have been eaten up." Next day she tracked her. Then she saw where she had gathered the clover. She looked all about there. She could not even find blood. Then she whistled. She heard nothing. Again she whistled. Again she did not hear anything. She went on and whistled again.

Then from a distance she heard a faint answer. "Ah, that is where my grandchild is," she said. Then she went there. She looked all over the clover. She could not find anything. She whistled again. It answered right by her. Then she saw blood there on the clover leaves. She took the bloody leaves and brought them home. Putting the blood in a basket, she took it to the spring and left it there, covering it with another basket. Then she went back to the house. Next day she went to look at it. She listened. Then she heard a tapping noise. "Oh, my grandchild is already growing," she said. Then she took off the covering basket. She took him to the house. He was already a person when she brought him into the house. Then she lived there with the child. Once the boy went out doors. He came back, crying: "My grandmother, I saw something! I want to shoot it." Then she made arrows for her grandson. When she had finished them he went out. He saw a bird and shot it. He killed it. Then he came back and gave her the bird. She said: "That is very good, my grandson." Again he went out and came back, saying: "My grandmother, I saw something. It has something on the top of its head." "It is a quail," she told him. Then the boy went and shot it. He came back and gave it to her. Then he said: "My bow is not good. Make me another one, a better one." Then Mikiti made him a good bow. She pulled out her pubic hair to make the bowstring. He went off again. He came back and said: "I saw something, grandmother." "What is it?" she asked. "This one has a longer crest." "That is a mountain quail. Go kill it." So the boy went off again. He came to the mountain quail and shot and killed it. Then he brought it back and gave it to his grandmother. He was still growing. Now he did not like his bow any longer. Once he said: "Is none of the property of my relatives left?" Then Mikiti told him: "Yes, there is some." "I would like to see it," he said. So she opened the house in which they had lived. Now there were all kinds of good fighting bows and fighting arrows and blankets and other things here. Then the boy went inside, and his grandmother told him: "Pick out what you want and take it." He said: "Yes, I will take this bow and these arrows." Now he tried all his arrows. Then his grandmother told him: "Do not go east from here; you will be killed if you do." Then he went off again. He went far east.

There he climbed on a rock. Then he went back to the house. He told his grandmother: "I went far east." She said: "Do not go there again. The grizzly bear will kill you." He said: "Oh, he cannot do anything. I will kill the old fellow with the big feet." Then he went off there once more. He shouted. At once a grizzly bear came out. He came close to the boy. Then the boy told him: "Go back! Run off! I do not want you." Again he shouted. Then at once another grizzly bear came. He also rushed up to the boy. Then the boy told him also: "Go back! Run! I do not want you," and the bear returned. Then he immediately shouted again. "Ah, you are the one I want," he said, as another grizzly came out. The bear said: "It is good," and at once jumped at him. The boy dodged him. Again the bear jumped. Then the boy jumped on the high rock. From there he shot the bear as he looked up. He shot him in the throat. Thus he killed him who had killed his mother. He skinned him. Then he went back. There was a rock at the place where Mikiti used to let water. He covered this rock with the bear skin. Then he went to the house. "Grandmother, go get water," he said. "Very well, my grandson," she said. Then she went to get water. She came there. She saw the bear skin. Then she ran back. As she ran along the path she urinated into her basket, dozhozhozhozhozhozh. Then she gave him what she had in her basket. The boy did not like it. He said: "This is not good water. Throw it away. Go get some good water." Then she went again. Again she saw the bear skin at the water and ran off without having brought water. As she went she urinated, and again brought her urine to the boy. He said: "You have not yet got good water." Then he told her: "Grandmother, why are you afraid where our water is? That is the skin of the bear that killed my mother."

The old woman, the girl, and the boy were all Mikiti. Every night they still cook acorns at this spring. In the morning the rocks are warm. But they cannot be seen and leave no tracks. They lived in the Paleuyami country and talked Paleuyami dialect.

YAUDANCHI YOKUTS. THE VISIT TO THE DEAD[34]

A woman died. Her husband went to where she was buried. At night he slept there. The next night he went and slept there. The next night he slept there again. Then in the middle of the night his wife came out of the grave. She stood tip and brushed the earth from herself. She faced north, not looking at him, and brushed herself entirely clean. She brushed her hair clean. Then she went north (khushim, actually somewhat west of north, in a direction at right angles to the prevailing course of the streams). Her husband followed her. They went on during the night. Then the dead woman turned into a log. At night she arose and brushed herself. Then they went on again. Then she turned to a log again. Again she got up and brushed herself and again they went on. Then they came to the bridge of the world of the dead (chedangdu wa tibiknicha). There the woman crossed. Her husband was unable to. On the other side were watchmen. They saw the man across the water. Then the watchmen were told to make a bridge for him. Then he crossed. The watchmen smelled of him. They told him: "Sit there." Then he sat in that place. The watchmen knew how he felt. They said: "Perhaps he is hungry. Give him something to eat." Then they gave him one pinenut. He ate the pinenut. Then there were more in his hand. He ate these and again there were more. At last he was satisfied. At night the people there danced. Next day they again danced at night. Then the watchmen told him: "Take away the woman." They said to her: "It will be well if you too go back." Then they started. But they told him: "Do not sleep." Now they went. They spent a night on the way. They went on again. Again they spent the night. They went another day. Then at night he slept. Then he was lying with a log.

YAUDANCHI YOKUTS. THE MAN AND THE OWLS. A TALE

A Waksachi (a Shoshonean tribe on the Kaweah drainage) man and his wife were traveling. They camped over night in a cave. They had a fire burning. Then they heard a horned owl (hutulu) hoot. The woman said to her husband: "Call in the same way. He will come and you can shoot him and we will eat him for supper." The man got his bow and arrows ready and called. The owl answered. He called again and again and the owl answered, coming nearer. At last it sat on a tree near the fire. The man shot. He killed it. Then his wife told him: "Do it again. Another one will come." Again he called and brought an owl and shot it. He said. "It is enough now." But his wife said: "No. Call again. If you call them in the morning they will not come. We have had no meat for a long time. We shall want something to eat to-morrow as well as now." Then the man called. More owls came. There were more and more of them. He shot, but more came. It was full of them all about. All his arrows were gone. The owls came closer and attacked them. The man took sticks from the fire and fought them off. He covered the woman with a basket and kept on fighting. More and more owls came. At last they killed both the man and the woman.

YAUELMANI YOKUTS. THE BEGINNING OF THE WORLD

AT first there was water everywhere. A piece of wood (wichet, stick, wood, tree) grew up out of the water to the sky. On the tree there was a nest. Those who were inside did not see, any earth. There was only water to be seen. The eagle was the chief of them. With him were the wolf, Coyote, the panther, the prairie falcon, the hawk called po'yon, and the condor. The eagle wanted to make the earth. He thought: "We will have to have land." Then he called k'uik'ui, a small duck. He, said to it: "Dive down and bring up earth." The duck dived, but did not reach the bottom. It died. The eagle called another kind of duck. He told it to dive. This duck went far down. It finally reached the bottom. Just as it touched the mud there it died. Then it came up again. Then the eagle and the other six saw a little dirt under its finger nail. When the eagle saw this he took the dirt from its nail. He mixed it with telis and pele seeds and ground them up. He put water with the mixture and made dough. This was in the morning. Then he set it in the water and it swelled and spread everywhere, going out from the middle. (These seeds when ground and mixed with water swell.) In the evening the eagle told his companions: "Take some earth." They went down and took a little earth up in the tree with them. Early in the morning, when the morning star came, the eagle said to the wolf: "Shout." The wolf shouted and the earth disappeared, and all was water again. The eagle said: "We will make it again," for it was for this purpose that they had taken some earth with them into the nest. Then they took telis and pele seeds again, and ground them with the earth, and put the mixture into the water, and it swelled out again. Then early next morning, when the morning star appeared, the eagle told the wolf again: "Shout!" and he shouted three times. The earth was shaken by an earthquake, but it stood. Then Coyote said: "I must shout too." He shouted and the earth shook a very little. Now it was good. Then they came out of the tree on the ground. Close to where this tree stood there was a lake. The eagle said: "We will live here." Then they had a house there and lived there.

Now every evening when the sun went down tokho (sokhon, tobacco) came there and went into the water in the lake. Coyote wanted to catch it. The eagle asked him: "How will you do it?" Coyote said: "Well, I will do it." He went off into the brush, rolled string on his thigh, and made it into a snare, which he put into the water. Tokho came, entered the water, and was caught. Coyote tried to take hold of it, but it was too hot. He could not touch it. It was like fire. Only after the sun came up was he able to take hold of it. Now, after he had held it all night, the tokho said to him: "Take me to the house." Coyote asked it: "What does tokho mean?" It said: "I am tobacco (sokhon). Give me to the prairie falcon." Coyote brought it to the house and said: "Who wants this?" The eagle did not want it. None of the seven wanted it except the prairie falcon. He said: "I will take it." Coyote asked it: "What are you good for?" The tobacco said: "I am good for many things. If there is anything you want to have, use me, and then whatever it is that you wish will be so." The prairie falcon said: "I will try it." At night he took a little of the tobacco in his mouth and blew out: "Pu! I want it to rain." Then it began to rain. It rained all night.

Then Coyote said: "We will make a woman of a deer." Then they killed a deer. They put it under a blanket of tules. It was entirely covered. When the morning star came it got up. It was a person (yokots) now. It was a woman. Coyote said: "I will sleep with her." That night he slept with her. In the morning he was dead. The woman was not hurt. The prairie falcon took a sharp water-grass (kapi). He said: "Stick it in his anus and he will get up." One of them put it in. Coyote got up hurriedly. "Ah, I was sleepy," he said. He said: "That is not good. It is not sweet. All men will die. We shall have to do it differently." Then he killed her. He left her under the blanket over night. Then he said: "To-night I will try it again." Then he slept with her. In the morning he got up early. "This is all right," he said. "This is good. We will let it be like that." This is how people came to be: deer was the mother. They made her by means of tobacco, blowing (spitting) it out while they said what they wished. But the prairie falcon ate nothing but tobacco. He lived on that. Thus the earth was made.

YAUELMANI YOKUTS. THE ORIGIN OF DEATH

IT was Coyote who brought it about that people die. He made it thus because our hands are not closed like his. He wanted our hands to be like his, but kondjodji (a lizard), said to him: "No, they must have my hand." He had five fingers and Coyote had only a fist. So now we have an open hand with five fingers. But then Coyote said: "Well, then they will have to die."

YAUELMANI YOKUTS. COYOTE'S ADVENTURES AND THE PRAIRIE FALCON'S BLINDNESS

THEY were living at Kamupau (south of San Emidio, which is at the end of the San Joaquin valley). Coyote's son was the hummingbird. He gambled constantly and won from everybody. Then the eagle, the chief, said: "Coyote's son is bad. We will kill him." They went to the owl, huhuwet, to have him make a fire which would burn up the hummingbird. They made the jackrabbit take this fire inside himself. Next day the crow went to Coyote and said to him: "Let us hunt." When they were hunting, he said to Coyote's son: "Shoot that jackrabbit there!" When the boy was about to shoot, his father told him: "Do not miss the little white mark on his forehead." The boy shot and caused a great fire to start. Coyote called to his son: "Come," and they ran. The fire followed them rapidly, trying to overtake them. They went up on a bare white mountain in the northeast. After three days the fire stopped burning. It had burned the mountains. Then Coyote said: "I will go back to see about our property. You must stay here until I come back." Then Coyote went back to Kamupau. He arrived there at night. The crow looked and saw a fire in Coyote's house. Then he told the eagle: "Coyote is alive still. We did not kill him." In the morning they went to him. "Where have you been?" they said. Coyote said: "I was lost." The eagle told him: "It is well. Everything is as it used to be." "Very well," said Coyote. Now one day Coyote began to carry wood and lay it outside his house. For three days he worked bringing wood. Then the people began to say: "What is Coyote doing? He has been bringing wood for three days. What is it for? He must be crazy." Then Coyote went off. He traveled one night. He came to the moon. The moon said to him: "What do you want, my elder brother?" Coyote said: "I have come to see you." What for?" asked the moon. Coyote said: "I will tell you what I want. I do not want you to rise any more. Stay at home." The moon said: "Very well. But you had better go to see my brother." Then Coyote went to see his brother, the thunder. "What do you want?" he asked. Coyote said: "I will tell you." "Well, tell me," said the thunder. Coyote said: "My brother, I do not want you to appear. Stay back where I want you to." "Well, yes," said the thunder; "but you had better go to our other brother. See what he says. He will do what is right." Then Coyote went to see the sun. He went into the house. The sun did not want to see him. He turned away from him. Coyote spoke to him but he turned away as if he were angry. Three times Coyote spoke. Then the sun turned and said: "What do you want?" Coyote said: "I want you to stay here and not to travel." "Very well," said the sun; "is that all you want?" "Yes," said Coyote. "Very well," said the sun, "go to see our brother the night. He will tell you what he will do." Then Coyote went to where the night was, far off in the last land. When Coyote came there it was dark and he could not see. "Where are you," he said. No one answered. "Where are you?" he said. Still there was no answer. "Where are you?" he asked. Then it began to be light. "What do you want?" he was asked. "I want you not to come about but to stay here," said Coyote. "Very well; is that all?" asked the night. "Yes." Then the night asked him: "When do you want me to do this?" Coyote said: "I will shout three times. You will hear it." "Well, shout loudly," said the night, and Coyote agreed. Then he went back to Kamupau. He arrived at night. In the morning he got up early, shouted, shouted again, and shouted again three times. It remained night, foggy and drizzling, and the sun did not rise.[35] People sat up, became tired, lay down again, and slept. Coyote lived well. He had much food and plenty of wood. So it was for a month. Then the people said: "What is it? Where is the sun?" "I do not know," they told each other. "Go to see Coyote," the eagle said. "Perhaps he has done it. Bring him these beads." Then the crow went. He told Coyote: "The chief sends you these. He wants you to take them. What have you done?" Coyote said: "I do not know. I cannot do anything." The crow went back. "What did he say?" the eagle asked him. "He said he could do nothing." Now none of the people had any wood. All around the houses there was water. It had rained for three months and was dark constantly and there was no sun nor moon. Then the crow came again to Coyote. "What is the matter?" he said. "There is no sun nor moon, there is nothing. The chief wants you to make it better." Coyote said: "I do not know how. Perhaps it is that they just have not come of themselves." The crow went back and said: "He says he does not know. He will not help. I think he does not want to. He does not wish them to come." Coyote was still living well, with plenty of wood and plenty of food. The people were in the water. The grass was high. It had rained four months now. They were without food or fire. Two months more they endured it. Then they went to Coyote again with a great quantity of beads (lilna), three sacks full. The crow gave them to Coyote. Coyote said: "What do you want? Food or wood?" The crow said: "The chief wants the weather changed. What is wrong with this world that there is no sun and no moon?" Coyote told him: "I do not know. I will try." Then he gave six sacks of beads to the eagle, double of what he had received. So he outdid the eagle. He said: "I will see what I can do." The crow took the six sacks of beads. When he gave them to the eagle, this one asked him: "What did he say?" The crow told him: "He said: 'I will try.'" Then Coyote went to the moon. For six months it had been night now, for one-half a year. The moon said: "Well, you have come." Coyote said: "Yes, I want you to travel again now." "Very well," said the moon. Then Coyote went to the thunder. "You have, come," he said. "Yes. I want you to appear again." Then he went to the sun, and told him also. "Travel again now," and the sun agreed.

Then he went to the night and told him. "Come back to your place now." "Very well; when?" Coyote said: "I will shout three times. You will hear me." Then he went back. He shouted, and shouted, and shouted a third time. Soon it cleared and became light. The sun came, and people saw grass and clover, and ate. They thought much of Coyote because he had brought this about.

Soon Coyote started out again. He said: "I am going to see my son. I shall come back soon." The chief told him: "Very well, but come back at once without staying. We want you here." Coyote agreed and started. He went towards the white mountain where his son was. He went up Kern river past Bakersfield to Gonoilkin, a waterfall. There he sat and looked at the river. He saw many fish and wanted to eat them. Then he said:

epash epash epash wanil wanil wanil
fish fish fish come come come

habak [1] tutsuat [2] tsenil [3]
approach-the-fire [1] a-plant [2] ? [3]

Soon little fish came to him. "You are no epash fish," he said and threw them back into the river. Then he called again. Soon fish came that were a little larger, but he threw them back also, saying: "You are no epash fish." He called again, and this time they came as big as his forearm. He picked them up and threw them back, telling them: "You are no epash fish." Then he called once more and they came as big as his thigh. Then he said: "Ya epash, ma epash, now they are epash fish, you are epash fish." He kept on calling and more came. He filled a large hole in the rock with them. Then he carried them to Wakhachau. He said: "I think I will cook them here. No, I think I will not. I will go down below. It is sandy here and not a good place." He went down the river to Woilo, at Bakersfield. He did not like it there and went on again down the river to Kuyo. He did not like it there and went to Pokhalin tinliu. He did not like it there either and went on to Tashlibunau, San Emidio. Now he had carried them a long way. He said: "There is plenty of wood here. I will cook." There was a big hole. In this he made his fire. Then he thought: "If I put them entirely into this they will burn." So he put their heads into the hole and covered them up, leaving only the tails sticking out lying one next to the other all around. So they cooked. He sat there. Then he said: "I have bododiwat (small black ill-smelling beetles) inside of me. I have good meat in my belly, I will mix my food. I will drink and make it salty." Then he went to a clear, bitter creek. Of that he drank. He drank too much of it. He went back to where his fish were cooking. Soon he was taken with colic. He defecated. Then he saw the bododiwat and laughed. He said: "There is my good mixed meat." He went back to where his fish were. Soon he defecated again. He laughed again at seeing the beetles. "There is that good meat. I am well now. I have put it outside of me. It will not be mixed any more." Now he was weak. He could not walk or get up. He had defecated too much. He could hardly sit up. He began to roll, and rolled like a log into the river. There he stayed until he became well. Then he got up and went where his fish were. He sat down. He said: "Well, I will eat now." He dug up the earth, took the loose tails, and threw them away, all around, here and there. He dug and dug, but there was nothing else there. He said: "What is the matter? Perhaps I have cooked them too much and they have gone down into the ground." He dug away but found no fish. He said: "They must have cooked so much that they went down further." He dug and dug until he was tired. He tore up the rocks and pulled them out. He got no fish, but he made a big hole. Soon batlawu (a red-headed fish-eating bird) came to Coyote. He asked: "What are you looking for?" Coyote said: "I am looking for my fish. Who took them?" Batlawu said: "I will tell you who took them." Coyote said: "I will give you half if you tell me." Batlawu told him: "You will see him soon. He is in the woods up here." It was sokhsukh (a fish-eating bird) who had stolen the fish. He had eaten them all. Coyote came to him. He said: "Give me half." Sokhsukh shook his head and vomited half the fish. Coyote ate that. Then he said: "Now I will call you and kill you." He called: "Sokhsukh!" and sokhsukh fell. Coyote tried to catch him but he escaped. Again he tried to seize him but he escaped. Soon he flew up so high that Coyote could not reach him any longer. He still followed him, looking up at him. They traveled over half the land from the hills down to the lake (Tulare lake). Then sokhsukh disappeared. Coyote could not see him any longer. Then he stopped. "It is too far to go back to the hills," he said. "I will go to the lake. I can eat tules and mud. It will be good." Then he went to the lake. He was hungry. Then he ate tule (-roots). He said: "It is well. Now I will go to see what I can find." He went. He saw many ducks. He said: "I will kill many of them. Then I shall be well off." So he started to hunt them. The ducks were calling: "en, en, en" Coyote listened, still thinking: "I will kill them and eat them." He went on again. The ducks continued to call: ("en, en, en") Coyote danced to the sound. Suddenly he danced into the water and the ducks flew up. He went on again until he found more ducks in the lake. He thought: "I will try to kill them. If I am lucky I shall kill one or two of them, and then I shall have something to eat." He approached them. The ducks heard him coming and sang: ""en, en, en" Coyote began to dance again and danced into the water. The ducks flew up.

Coyote said: "I cannot kill them. I will let it be." Then he went on until he came north of Tulamni. There he saw a man looking into the water. He was wa'k (a bird). He had many small fish. Coyote went to him. The man asked him: "What are you doing here?" Coyote said: "Nothing. I came to see you. I want to eat of the fish you have caught." The man said: "Well, take some.

There is what I have caught." Coyote ate of them. He ate them raw, bones and all. Then he said: "I will go on now." The man asked him: "Where are you going?" Coyote said: "I am going to see my son." The man said: "You will see a man below here who will give you more fish." Coyote went on down and saw a man sitting. It was wakhat, the crane. He reached him. "Hello!" he said. "Hello! Where are you going?" asked the crane. Coyote said: "I came to see you. I want to eat of the fish you are catching." "Very well," said the crane. Coyote ate. He ate them raw, he was so hungry (or, greedy). "Where are you going?" asked the crane. "I am going to see my son," said Coyote. The crane told him: "You will see another man fishing." Coyote went on. Then he saw many men fishing, batlawu and yimelan (a diving bird). Coyote said: "Hello! Are you here?" They said: "Yes." He said: "I have come to eat of your fish." They said: "Very well, there are many in there. Eat as many as you want." Then Coyote made a fire in the place and ate. He ate all he wanted. When he had enough, he said: "Why do you not go over there? There are many large fish there. I was there a long time. ago." He was lying. They said: "Show us how to catch them." Coyote said: "Very well. But show me how you make your noses red." They told him: "We put tule into the hot ashes and then put it on our noses and it makes them red." Coyote said: "It is good. I wish you would do it to me." "Very well," they said. Then they put Coyote into the ashes and glowing tules. Three or four of them held him down. He was burned in the fire and died. "Throw him away. He is no good," they said, and then went off. Coyote lay there. Next day he woke up. He said: "I have been asleep. Where did they go to?" Now his nose was white. The flesh had come off and the bone showed. Then he came to those who had done this to him. 'You have been asleep," they said. "Yes, I slept a little," he said. "How is it that you are red and I am white?" "You burned it too much," they said; "you are redder than we are." They had got a rock ready so that it looked like a dakhdu fish. They said: "Here is a dakhdu (a large fish with spines on its back). You have a large month, ours are little. See if you can catch it." Coyote said: "Well, I will go and see." Then they went to the place to dive. Coyote jumped in, struck the rock, and mashed his head, which was already only bones. He died again. They left him and went off. Next day Coyote got up and looked around. No one was there. He went on. He said: "Well I think I must go to the place for which I started." He went on and on but saw no one. Then he came to where there were many men. They asked him: "Where have you been?" He told them: "Oh, about the land." They asked: "Where are you going?," He said: "I am going to see my son." They said: "It is well." Then he told them: "I want to stay here for a time. I am tired." The chief said: "Very well."

Next day they began to gamble. People there gambled all the time. Now the prairie falcon had been gambling and had lost one of his eyes. "I want to win your other eye," his opponent said. The prairie falcon agreed and they played again. Then, when it was nearly sunset the prairie falcon had lost both his eyes. Then he took a sharp grass that grows on the mountains and cut out his eyes and gave them to the man who had won them. Now he sat there. Then his friend the crow came to him and said: "We had better go into the house." The prairie falcon said: "No, I will not go into the house." The crow asked Min: "What are you going to do? Will you sit here all night?" He said: "Well, I am going north. I have a relative (nusus, father's sister) there." In the middle of the night he started. He had no eyes. The crow said: "I will go with you." "Very well," he said. Then he sang a little as they started to go.

khoyu nan	return (= bad luck comes to?)
ama, nim huwut	me
t'awe nan	then my gambling

dokoi nim	beat me
	gambling-implements my

So he sang and started. He went singing all the time. After a longtime he said: "Are you hungry?" The crow said: "Yes." "Where is there a bush?" "Here," said the crow. The prairie falcon felt around until he touched the bush. Suddenly he struck it and killed a rabbit. Then the crow ate. When he had finished, the prairie falcon asked him: "Do you want water?" The crow said: "Yes." The prairie falcon told him: "Turn the other way around," and the crow turned. Soon the prairie falcon said to him: "Well, now you can turn this way." The crow turned around and there was a little spring there. The prairie falcon had made it for him. Then he drank and they went on. Now they came to a village. A man said: "What is the matter with the prairie falcon? He is blind. A man holds him by the band and leads him. It is the crow, his friend." The prairie falcon sang: "Hiwèti, yona, hiwèti, naamtayo, lanîyo, hilalèkiyo, tawatè" They stayed at that village one night. Then they went on again. Again the prairie falcon asked his companion: "Are you hungry?" and when the crow said that he was, he did the same as before. He struck a bush and killed a rabbit and the crow cooked it and ate it. Then he asked him: "Do you want to drink?" and again made a spring for him. From there they went on again. They came to a village. The people said: "What is the matter with the prairie falcon? He is blind and his friend the crow is leading him by the hand." They asked him: "What is the matter?" He said: "I have lost my eyes gambling." The chief said: "It is too bad. Where are you going now?" He said: "I am going to my relative." The chief asked him: "Will you stay here?" He said: "Yes, for a little while." The chief said to him: "We would like you to sing." "Very well," he said. Then he sang: "Yahilulu-mai, yahimai lulmnai, sawawa kanama, taniyo, yapiwi piwimai, tawana tsiniyo, hilalikiyo, tawati tawat." The prairie falcon and the crow went on again from that place. They went far. Again he asked the crow: "Are you hungry?" and killed a rabbit and made water for him. He himself ate nothing. He only used tobacco. That was his food. Then they came to a village. (The same conversation is repeated). Then he sang for them: "Hilamata, hayaawiyu, lokoyowani, waatin, humuyu hile." It was at Kaweah that he sang thus. In the morning they went on again. The traveled far. Then they came to Chowchilla. They approached a village. (The same dialogue is repeated.) "Stay here and sing," they said and he agreed. He sang: "Hosimi, hosiwimine, wanit wilima, lananama, hosimi." That is the end. The prairie falcon stayed there.

YAUELMANI YOKUTS. THE PRAIRIE FALCON LOSES

AT Kamupau, south of San Emidio, many people lived. The eagle was the chief. Coyote was there too. He was a good talker and knew everything. The prairie falcon was there. He was fierce. The large owl, hutulu, and the small ground owl, tokowets, both of them medicine-men, were there. The panther was there. He was a good hunter. The weasel, the fox, and the magpie lived there too. These three were all gamblers. Many others lived there. Every day the hunters, the eagle, the prairie falcon and the panther, went out for rabbits. Coyote brought wood to every house. He never went hunting. When the hunters came back they called to Coyote: "Tutunusut!" That was his name. They gave him the intestines of the rabbits and he ate them. They also gave him the unborn rabbits (wasis). When Coyote received these he spoke over them and blew on them and made them larger (sukhua, to make or create by blowing). By the time he came to his house they were large rabbits. In this way he lived. The gamblers played every day at the gambling ground with the hoop and poles. Now the small black-eared rabbit, tukuyun, came from pitnani (the forks of Kern river, the country of the Shoshonean Pitanisha or Tübatulabal). Coyote said: "A stranger has come." They went to him and brought him into the chief's house. He was bringing food with him, pinenuts, and puhuk, and hapu. This he gave to the eagle. Next morning he went to gamble with the fox. The rabbit won everything. He won also the weasel's beads. He won all that the magpie had. He won everything from all the gamblers. Coyote was about as an attendant. He helped them as they played and was paid for it. He did not ask to receive much. He did not expect to be made rich. In the evening they stopped playing because the rabbit had won everything. Early in the morning they began again. Now the rabbit gambled with the prairie falcon. The prairie falcon won everything he had. He won all that the rabbit had won the day before as well as the beads which the eagle had given him for the food which he had brought. Then the rabbit told him: "I have nothing more." But the prairie falcon said to him: "Play for your ear." The rabbit agreed. Then they played and the prairie falcon won his ear. He cut it off. "Try with the other," he said, and the rabbit consented. The n Coyote said to the rabbit: "Wait." Then he went off to the wife of the prairie falcon, who was in the house making a basket. He told her: "I want my gambling hoop. It is in the bed." The woman said: "I cannot find it." Coyote went there and found it. Then he cohabited with the woman. Then the prairie falcon began to lose. The rabbit won everything back again. He won everything that he had lost. He won everything that the prairie falcon had. Then the prairie falcon thought: "To-night I must go away and die. I have nothing left." That night he went off toward the coast. In the morning he was in the hills. He saw smoke. He went to the house there. An old woman and a girl were there. They took him in. The old woman got up and gave him acorn soup and fish to eat. Then the prairie falcon was married again. He married that girl. At night two boys came fighting. They were the girl's brothers. As they fought outside the house, the old woman went out and told them: "Be quiet. Your brother-in-law is inside. It is the prairie falcon." They laughed and fought; then they came in and ate. Then the old woman told them to go outside again. They went out. Early in the morning they went to the ocean to fish. The prairie falcon went out into the brush and set snares for rabbits. He filled two sacks with rabbits and came home while it was still morning. At night the two boys came again and ate of the rabbits. They said: "Our brother-in-law has killed game. We will eat it. He is a good hunter. In the morning we will take him with us to catch fish." Then the girl said: "Are you going fishing in the morning?" The prairie falcon said: "Yes, I will go." In the morning they went. They went in a boat out on the ocean. They caught fish and filled the boat. Then the wind blew the boat out to sea. The two boys (by sukhua, magic by blowing) then created a string with which they pulled the boat back to land. Next day the prairie falcon went fishing again with his brothers-in-law. They caught many fish and filled the boat. Now the wind came and blew them out to sea again. Then the prairie falcon fell into the water and drowned. The 'two boys fought in the boat because their brother-in-law was dead. When they came to land they fought again. Then they went home.

Now Coyote, another coyote who was the prairie falcon's mother's brother, knew that he was dead. He knew it because he had supernatural power (tipni). He was in the house with his wife. When the prairie falcon died he felt bad. His heart came out of his mouth, he felt so sorry. He would have died, but he caught his heart as it was in the air and put it back into his month. Then he went to where the prairie falcon's new wife was. "Where is the prairie falcon?' he asked the old woman. Then the two boys took him where the prairie falcon bad died. "Where did he fall in?" Coyote asked. "Here," they said. Then he took tobacco and dived far down into the water. He carne to seven trails. He could not tell which way to go. Then he took his tobacco and by means of it chose one trail. He followed this and came to a large communal house (gawi). There he saw a man with his knees burning. "You are burning," he said. He did riot answer. Coyote took tobacco, spoke over it, and made the person able to talk again. The prairie falcon was in the house. Only his feathers were left. Now he sang in the Tokye (Chumash) language: "Kapikh, tata, shakhshaniwash, salialama. You came, my uncle. You will die." Then Coyote sang also. He sang: "I am dead already. You know it." He meant that he should have died when he had jumped into the water, and therefore could not really die. Then he took the prairie falcon. No one was there except the old man whose knees were being burned for wood. So Coyote took the prairie falcon back with him. Then he put blue rock-paint on him as medicine and made him well again. This was through his supernatural power. He took a small sharp grass and stuck him in the anus. Then the prairie falcon got up.

The girl, the old woman, and the two boys were spiders of a species called ulumush or kolokilwi. The prairie falcon's uncle, Coyote, came from Nohomo, southwest of San Emidio.

GITANEMUK SHOSHONEAN. THE PANTHER'S CHILDREN AND COYOTE

Told by a Yauelmani Yokuts

TWO women lived alone. One was a woman and the other a girl. The old woman was the jimson weed; the girl the cottontail rabbit. They lived west above Tejon creek. In the morning the old woman saw a dead deer lying at the door. She did not see who brought it. She took the deer, sliced it, dried the meat, and said nothing. She did not ask the girl about it. Next day the same thing happened. Three times it happened. Then the girl gave birth to two boys, twins. They saw no one. She did not see her husband. The boys grew up and she put them into a cradle. Coyote lived at Sututaiwieyau and had seven sons. He said: "I will go to see what they are doing." The mother of the two boys was on the plain gathering seeds. The old woman was caring for the children. Coyote carne to the house. He found that they had plenty of deer meat and acorn mush. The old woman said to him: "Will you have meat and acorn mush?" He said: "Yes." Then she gave him. the food and he ate. After eating he was thirsty. She told him: "There is water in the pitched basket (made with piñon gum)." Coyote said: "I do not drink from that kind. The pitch stinks." She told him: "What kind do you drink from?" He said: "I drink from an openwork winnowing basket (khali)." She asked him: "How does it hold water?" He said: "Put leaves into it." The old woman went and tried to bring water in an openwork basket. The water kept running out, but she kept trying a long time. Meanwhile Coyote took the two boys and went off, making a circuit. The mother was far off on the plain gathering seeds. At night she came home. "Where are my boys?" she asked her mother. The old woman said: "Coyote came here. I think he stole them." Now the panther came. "Where are the children?" he said. "Coyote stole them," they told him. He took pinenuts and puhuk and hapu in a sack and started to look for his children. He looked all over the country. He looked for them for ten years, for about twelve years. Now the boys were large enough to go out and hunt rabbits. Then Coyote told them: "Do not go far. A man may come here. He is bad. He will catch you and kill you." He was afraid their father would come. Next day the boys went on the mountain and killed a deer. Then one day they went to the top of the mountain Wachkiu. From there they looked down on the plain on the other side. When they had rested, they got up to go. The younger one was behind. Then he saw a man coming. He was dark all over with a little white on his breast. He said: "See, the one is coming of whom our father told us, the dangerous one." The panther called: "Where are you going? Stop. I am your father." Then the younger brother said: "Let us wait." They stopped. "Hello," said the anther. "Hello," they told him. He asked them: "Why do you run away? I am your father. Coyote is not your father." Then he took one by each hand and they went. Soon the old man became tired and fell. He got up again, took pinenuts and puhuk and hapu from his sack, and gave them to the boys to eat. They ate them all. Then he asked them: "How does he do when he kills deer!" They told him: "He eats all the intestines before he takes it home." Then their father told them: "Well, I will do that." Now he killed a deer. Then the boys went and called Coyote to come. They said they had killed a deer. Coyote came. "Whose track is that?" he said. The older boy said: "It is my track," and Coyote was satisfied. Then he went to the deer. He wanted to eat of it. He nearly bit at it when he jumped in fear. Three times he was afraid and jumped aside. Then he went to it and ate. Now the panther jumped on him, killed him, and tore him to pieces. He strewed his flesh over the ground. Then he went to the house. Coyote's children were playing in a swing. They did not work or hunt but played constantly. The panther killed them all. He took them by the feet and struck them on the ground. He entered the house where Coyote's wife was, took her by the feet, and threw her out. Then he burned the house and went off. He said: "I am going. I travel over the country."

ABSTRACTS

1. Rumsien Costanoan. Water covers the world. The humming-bird and Coyote are on Pico Blanco. They fly to the Sierra del Gabilan. The water subsides. Coyote finds a woman and by order of the eagle marries her. The manner of making children is discussed. Coyote makes his wife louse him and swallow what she finds. She becomes pregnant and runs away. He follows, vainly trying to delay her, until she throws herself into the ocean. (Cf. 7, 11, 15, 25, 37.)

2. Rumsien Costanoan. Coyote marries a second wife to have. more children. He sends the children out to found villages with different languages. He gives the people bow and arrows and instructs them how to gather and prepare food. He becomes old and goes away.

3. Rumsien Costanoan. Coyote vainly tries to kill the humming-bird. At last he swallows him, but the humming-bird scratches, him so that he is forced to let him out.

4. Rumsien Costanoan. Coyote takes his wife to the ocean after warning her not to be frightened at the sea animals. He forgets to tell her of one, which when it appears frightens the woman to death. Coyote restores her to life.

5. Rumsien Costanoan. Coyote wishing to keep his cooked salmon for himself, pretends to his children that he is eating ashes.

6. Rumsien Costanoan. Coyote, pretending to have a thorn in his eye, comes to women. When one of them tries to draw it, he runs off with her.

7. Pohonichi Miwok. At first there is only water. Coyote sends a duck to dive and it brings up earth, from which he makes the world, (Cf. 1, 11, 15, 25, 37.)

8. Pohonichi Miwok. The turtle, far in the mountains, alone has fire. Coyote turns himself into a piece of wood, is put into the fire, and runs off with it to the Miwok. (Cf. 16, 26.)

9. Pohonichi Miwok. On the first human death, Coyote wishes to revive the person, but the meadow lark, thinking there will be no room on the earth, prevails that men should die. Coyote institutes cremation of the dead. (Cf. 12, 17, 38.)

10. Pohonichi Miwok. The grizzly bear and the deer, two women, each have two children. The two women go out together and the grizzly bear kills the deer. The deer children kill the two bear children in a sweat-house, and flee from the grizzly bear to their grandfather. As she enters his sweat-house she is killed by his supernatural power. The two boys become thunders. (For the thunder twins, cf. 23. Cf. the Kwakiutl, Çatloltq, Thompson, Kathlamet, and Lutuami parallels cited by Dixon, 341; also Dixon, 49, and Powers, 341.)

11. Gashowu Yokuts. At the bidding of the prairie falcon various birds and water animals dive for earth when everything is water. A small cluck alone reaches the bottom. From a little sand left under his finger nail the prairie falcon, adding tobacco, makes the earth and the mountains by dropping the mixture into the water. The raven's mountains, now the Sierra Nevada, but then along the coast, being the larger, the prairie falcon interchanges them. (Cf. 1, 7, 15, 25, 37.)

12. Gashowu Yokuts. At a person's death it is resolved that after three days people are to return to life. The meadow lark, being newly married, dislikes the stench of the corpse and persuades the people to burn it. (Cf. 9, 17, 38.)

13. Gashowu Yokuts. Coyote's pretense to be a medicine man is exposed when he fails to revive the dead prairie falcon. The white owl brings him back to life.

14. Gashowu Yokuts. A woman, the hawk, lives alone and hides all the deer. The people hunt in vain. The wolf and Coyote find her and are given food. The people discover that their families are supplied with meat. The magpie, who has supernatural knowledge, informs the chief, the eagle. and the people all go to the woman, who is compelled to feed them. Many men wish to marry her, but all fail. They leave, but Coyote, pretending sickness, remains. By making a storm he persuades her to admit him into the house. She knows his thoughts and long resists his desires, but finally consents to marry him. She meets him with a rattlesnake, but is foiled by his use of a stick on which the rattlesnake is disabled.

The condor, the son of Coyote and the woman, is made to grow up quickly by being, immersed in water (cf. 34), and becomes a famous gambler. When traveling he aims at an owl, who, being a medicine man, sings and changes him into a condor who flies off. When Coyote returns his wife kills him with a rattlesnake. The condor lives in the sky, killing people for food. He carries up his mother and two little boys and a girl. He keeps the children to eat later. His mother instructs them. When he returns to drink for half a day and then to mount to the higher sky from which he will descend to kill them, they shoot at him. Half a day's shooting has no apparent effect and the woman and the children hide. The condor rises, but finally falls dead and is burnt. His eyes fly out, are lost in the brush, and turn to condors. The woman and the little girl return to earth on a feather rope. The two boys go south in the sky until they reach the earth. They come to people who can neither talk nor eat and who live by odor. The boys cut months and tongues for them and return home.

15. Truhohi Yokuts. The world is covered with water. A mountain top is the only land. The people eat this for food. The eagle, urged by Coyote, succeeds in having the mudhen bring up earth by diving. From this earth mixed with seeds, the world is made. The wolf is sent out to go around it. Coyote, though forbidden, also makes the circuit, and, breaking the soft ground in his journey, produces the mountains. The eagle sends the prairie falcon and the raven northward to make the mountain ranges. At first the Coast Range is higher than the Sierra Nevada. The eagle sends off the animals to different places to become people. (Usually in Indian myths the "first people" turn to animals. Cf. 32). The eagle himself rises to the sky. To his surprise Coyote follows him. (Cf. 1, 7, 11, 25, 37.)

16. Truhohi Yokuts. The crow, sent out by the eagle, succeeds in finding fire. The roadrunner, the fox, the crow, and Coyote go north, and when the people are asleep steal fire. Coyote delays to kill a child and is pursued. Turning in his flight, he makes the crooked course of the San Joaquin river. Reaching his sweat-house he is safe from pursuit. (Cf. 8, 26.)

17. Truhohi Yokuts. Two insects dispute whether people are to live or die. The one favoring death prevails. Coyote is satisfied because there will be festivities at mourning ceremonies. (Cf. 9, 12, 38.)

18. Truhohi Yokuts. People living in the Coast Range keep the sun. Coyote and the eagle take it away from them. The people turn to a circle of stones.

19. Tachi Yokuts. The antelope and deer race. Their course is the Milky Way. The antelope wins and lives in the plains. The deer goes into the brush. (Many and close eastern parallels. Cf. Pawnee and Blackfoot, by Grinnell; also Arapaho, Field Columbian Mus. Anthr. Ser. V, 16.)

20. Tachi Yokuts. The Pleiades are five girls who are in love with a flea. In summer he becomes sick and they leave him while he is asleep. He pursues and they rise to the sky. He follows them and is a star near them. (See footnote as to Yaudanchi version.)

21. Tachi Yokuts. The wolf gives his wife, the crane, and his children nothing to eat. She leaves him. He follows and tries to kill her. She stabs hint to the heart with her bill. She goes off with her two boys, and they become stars in the constellation Orion.

22. Tachi Yokuts. The bald eagle steals men's wives. When he takes the prairie falcon's, the latter pursues and kills him.

23. Tachi Yokuts. Two boys, twins, are abused by their parents because they are covered with sores. Their grandmother pities them. Their parents leave with the people during a famine. The boys catch an abundance of fish in a spring. They acquire supernatural power, turning to thunders. Their mother's brother visits them and finds them provided with food. Their parents come with other people and are killed. (Cf. No. 10 and the Yuki story given.)

24. Tachi Yokuts. A woman dies. Her husband stays by her grave. She arises from the ground and for six rights he follows her on her Journey to the island of the dead. He cannot cross the bridge to the island until permitted by the chief of that country. A bird, darting up to frighten him into falling off, fails. He sees the people dancing. During the night he is with his wife. In the morning she is a fallen tree. After six days the chief sends him home. He is told not to show himself for six days. After five days he comes out from concealment and tells the people his experiences. In the morning a rattlesnake bites him and he dies. Front him the people learn that the island is continually filling up with the dead. They are taken to bathe, when a bird frightens them and many turn to fish and birds. In this way room is made on the island for others that die. (Cf. 15.)

25. Wükchamni Yokuts. The world is covered with water, except for one small spot on which are the eagle and Coyote. They send the duck to dive to the bottom and it brings them earth. From this they make the world. They make six men and six women, whom they send out in different directions. Coyote, sent out by the eagle to see what the people do, reports that they are eating the earth. The eagle sends out the dove and it finds a grain of meal. From this the eagle makes seeds all over the earth, and the people live on these. (Cf. 1, 7, 11, 15, 37.)

26. Yaudanchi Yokuts. Fire is kept by a man in the plains to the west. The antelope and other animals steal it, but on their return the fire is always put out by rain. The jackrabbit burrows and holds the fire in his hands under his belly. (Cf. Ute, Journ. Am. Folk-lore, XIV, 259, 1901.) He returns successfully. (Cf. 8, 16.)

27. Yaudanchi Yokuts. The eagle is chief. The condor attempts to replace him. The eagle catches him from ambush and the condor acknowledges his supremacy. (Cf. the actual practice of the Plains tribes in catching eagles.)

28. Yaudanchi Yokuts. The eagle's son, though forbidden, goes over a hill where he meets people. Several girls abuse him. Coyote and the black-faced dog try to shoot him but fail. Having returned home, the eagle's son goes out again. This time he is fine in appearance and the girls fall in love with him. They follow him, but none are received by his grandmother except the woodpecker, who before had not abused him. The others strike her on the head and make it red. She throws fire and ashes at them, spotting them with red, black, and gray. The eagle's son goes over the hill once more and kills Coyote and the dog.

29. Yaudanchi Yokuts. The prairie falcon, traveling, comes to a village. He frightens the people, kills them, and hangs up their hair on trees.

30. Yaudanchi Yokuts. The prairie falcon leaves his wife in charge of Coyote, who sleeps, and she is carried to the sky by the condor. The lizard at last locates her and the fly finds her. The prairie falcon goes up and brings her back.

31. Yaudanchi Yokuts. The prairie falcon wins at playing. Coyote goes to a mountain and rolls himself down until he looks like the prairie falcon. He then goes to the prairie falcon's wife and cohabits with her. From that time the prairie falcon's opponents win back what they have lost. (Cf. 40.)

32. Yaudanchi Yokuts. The foothill people fight those of the plains. Coyote and the humming-bird are the leaders. They beat the plains people, but cannot kill a fish and the turtle. Coyote makes arrow points of his own leg bone and kills them both. Then the eagle sends off the people (to become animals; cf. 15), and each one tells how he will live. They go off and turn to animals.

33. Yaundanchi {sic} Yokuts. Thunder and Whirlwind both hide the other's son, but each succeeds in recovering his own.

34. Yaudanchi (?) Yokuts. A girl living alone with her mother goes too far to gather clover, and, disobeying her instructions, eats some. A grizzly bear devours her. Her mother finds a trace of blood where she has been killed, puts it in a basket, and, leaving it in a spring, finds a boy in it. She makes bows and arrows for her grandson, who kills birds of different kinds. He takes a good bow left by his dead relatives. He goes and shouts for the grizzly bear. Several come but he sends them back. When the one comes that has killed his mother, he kills him. He sets up the skin at the spring, and sends his grandmother to bring him water. She is frightened, runs, and brings him urine. He tells her what he has done.

35. Yaudanchi Yokuts. A woman dies. Her husband stays at her grave. His wife arises from the ground and he follows her for several nights. She crosses the bridge to the world of the dead. He cannot follow her until permitted by the guardians. He is hungry and is given one pinenut, which multiplies and satisfies him. (A common episode in American mythologies.) At night the people dance. He is told to return with his wife, but they are forbidden to go to sleep. The third night he sleeps, and in the morning lies beside a log. (Cf. 24.)

36. Yaudanchi Yokuts. A man and his wife pass the night in a cave. The man calls owls by hooting and shoots them. Having killed two, he wishes to stop, but his wife urges him to continue. The owls come in great numbers and attack them. He resists, but finally both are killed.

37. Yauelmani Yokuts. The world is covered with water. In a nest on a tree (upright wood) arising from the water, are the eagle and six others, including Coyote. The eagle sends ducks to (live and finally receives earth. Mixing this with seeds, he makes the world. In the morning the eagle tells the wolf to shout. The earth disappears. They make the world over again. When the wolf shouts in the morning, there is an earthquake, but the earth remains. Coyote wishes to shout also, but the earth scarcely trembles. Now they live on the earth. Every evening tobacco enters the water. Coyote makes a snare and catches it. It is burning like fire. It says that if used its power is to bring anything to pass that is desired. (This episode resembles a Yurok myth of the origin of obsidian.) The prairie falcon uses the tobacco and on the first trial makes rain. Coyote kills a deer and makes a woman of it. Being killed by his first cohabitation with her, he is revived by the prairie falcon. He makes her over and is successful. (Cf. 1, 7, 11, 15, 25.) The prairie falcon lives from tobacco alone (like the Yurok hero Pulekukwerek).

38. Yauelmani Yokuts. Coyote wants human hands to be closed like his, but the lizard prevails and people have hands with fingers. Then Coyote makes it that people die. (Cf. 9, 17. For the incident of the hand, cf. Maidu, Bull. Am. Mus. Nat. Hist. XVII, 42; Yana, Creat. Myths Prim. Am., 479; also Yuki, etc.)

39. Yauelmani Yokuts. The humming-bird, Coyote's son, wins at gambling, and the people try to kill him by causing a great fire. Coyote and his son escape to a distant mountain. Coyote returns. He gathers wood. He travels to the moon, thunder, sun, night, and persuades them not to come. He returns and for six months there is no light and constant rain. Finally Coyote, returning the eagle's gifts, consents to bring back the sun. He visits the same powers as before, and when he shouts they reappear.

Coyote starts to visit his son. He catches fish but rejects all except the biggest. Going on, he cooks them all. He drinks alkali water and becomes sick. When he returns to his cooking, he finds only the tails. A bird has eaten the fish. Coyote finds him and asks for half the fish. The bird vomits them. Coyote tries to kill him but after following him a long time loses him. He comes to Tulare lake and tries to kill ducks. They quack and he dances to the sound until he falls into the water. He comes to a bird that gives him fish, and then to another. He comes to other birds and asks to have his nose made red. They hold him in the fire until he is dead. He returns to life and rejoins them. They tell him to dive for what appears to be a fish. He jumps into the water and is dashed to death on a rock. He comes to life and goes on. He reaches a village where he stays.

The people there gamble. The prairie falcon loses everything. (Cf. 31, 40.) He stakes his eyes and loses them. At night, accompanied by his friend the crow, he starts to go northward. As he goes he sings. When the crow becomes hungry and thirsty, he makes food and water for him. They spend the night in a village. They go on. The prairie falcon still sings. They reach another village. The third night they reach the Kaweah river. The fourth night they come to the Chowchilla.

40. Yauelmani Yokuts. Many people live together, with the eagle as chief. Coyote is servant. The prairie falcon is a successful gambler. The rabbit visits the people and wins all they have. Next day he gambles with the prairie falcon and loses everything. He loses one ear and stakes the second. Then Coyote goes to the prairie falcon's wife and cohabits with her. Now the prairie falcon loses everything that he has. (Cf. 31.) That night he goes off toward the coast. He comes to an old woman and a girl. He marries the girl. At night her two brothers, who constantly fight, come in. In the morning they go fishing and he catches rabbits. Next day he goes with them on the ocean. A wind blows the boat out to sea. The two boys by magic make a rope which draws them back to land. Next day the same thing happens, but the prairie falcon falls into the water and is drowned. Coyote, the prairie falcon's uncle, knows of his nephew's death by his heart trying to leave his body. The two boys show him where the prairie falcon fell into the water. Coyote dives down. Coming to seven trails he learns by means of his tobacco which to follow. He comes to a house "here he finds a man who is being burnt for fuel. The prairie falcon is there. Coyote takes him away and restores him to life.

41. Gitanemuk Shoshonean. A woman and her daughter live alone. Game is left at their door. After a time the girl gives birth to twins. She does not see her husband. Coyote comes there when the girl is away. He sends the old woman to get water in an openwork basket and steals the children. He brings them up. The panther, who is their father, cannot find them. The boys kill deer. Coyote has warned them against their father. They meet him. He hides and Coyote comes. The panther kills him. Then he kills Coyote's wife and children.

ENDNOTES

---

[1]XVIII, 85, 1905. (p. 2)

[2] See Journ. Am. Folk-Lore, XIX, 309, 1906. (p. 2)

[3] Bull. Am. Mus. Nat. Hist., XVII, 33-118, 1902. Compare also Some Coyote Stories from the Maidu Indians of California, Journ. Am. Folk-Lore, XIII, 267-270, 1900; System and Sequence in Maidu Mythology, ibid., XVI, 32-36, 1903; and Mythology, 333-342, of the Northern Maidu, Bull. Am. Mus. Nat. Hist., XVII, 119 seq. (p. 2)

[4] Boston, 1898. (p. 2)

[5] Elsewhere, p. 336, Dr. Dixon says that the creator placed small wooden figures in the ground, to grow into men at the end of the mythic era (p. 4)

[6] Tribes of California, Contrib. N. Am. Ethn. III: northern Maidu, 290, 292, 294; southern Maidu, 339, 341, 341, 342, 343, 344. (p. 6)

[7] Related to the myth about the wild-cat and panther's magical control of the deer, found among the Shasta (Burns), Yuki, and Lassik (Goddard) (p. 7)

[8] It appears accordingly that while the three stocks illustrated by the collections of Curtin and Dixon held the whole Sacramento valley region, the territory actually represented by the myths given in these collections comprises only a comparatively small part of the region, in a restricted area in northeastern California. This is a fact which must not be lost sight of in making comparisons. (p. 7)

[9] Bull. Am. Mus. Nat. Hist. XVII, 339, 340 (p. 10)

[10] Op. cit., 339, 340, 42. (p. 12)

[11] Op. cit., 273. (p. 12)

[12] Op. cit., 42, 71. (p. 12)

[13] Ibid., 335 (p. 12)

[14] Op. cit., 339 (p. 13)

[15] Land of Sunshine, XIV, 131, 132, 223, 310, 312, 397 (p. 13)

[16] From a half-breed informant, whose maternal grandfather was from Salmon river, her maternal grandmother from Scott's Valley. She lives at Forks of Salmon. The places mentioned in the myths are mostly on the Salmon and its two main forks; one is on New river, two on the Klamath in Karok territory, none in Scott's Valley (p. 13)

[17] Since the above was written Dr. Dixon has published in the American Anthropologist, n. s. VII, 607-12, 1905, an article discussing the mythology of the Shasta-Achomawi and its relation to the traditions of the neighboring peoples. No myths are given in detail, but the entire mythology is concisely summarized. Dr. Dixon finds considerable difference between the traditions of the Shasta and those of the Achomawi. He gives the creation of the latter much as it has been summarized above, except that Coyote is here said to have appeared from a cloud before the creator, the silver fox, arose from a fog. When the boat in which the two are drifting becomes worn out, the fox, while Coyote is asleep, combs out from his own body a mass of hair, forms it into a flat disk, sets it floating on the water, and on it places what are to be trees and plants. (This somewhat suggests the Yuki creation of the world from a basket.) After the making of mankind, the struggle between the creator and Coyote begins, Coyote wishing the conditions of life to be hard. He is successful, and death is brought into the world, although his own child is the first to die. The creator tries in vain to destroy Coyote. At this point the loon-woman myth is introduced. The animals, in trying to escape the loon, fall into

the fire kindled by her, and are burned to death. The fox, however, restores their hearts to life and gives to each animal its peculiar characteristics.

Among the Shasta the dualism between the creator and Coyote, which, although more philosophical, is on the whole less developed among the Achomawi than among the Maidu, is entirely lacking. The Achomawi creation {footnote p. 182} episodes are also wanting among the Shasta, and there is no clear idea of a creator or origin. The most that has been found is a confused account of a flood. After the subsidence of the water the world is largely shaped by the eagle, who sends a boy and a girl who marry and originate the human race. There is little trace of the making of animals or anything else. Coyote assumes a very important rôle, in that he names the animals. Although he is responsible for the introduction of death into the world, the story is told differently than by the Achomawi or Maidu. The systematic orderly character of the mythology, which the Achomawi share with the Maidu, is entirely lacking among the Shasta, and creation ideas are as absent as in Northwestern California.

In the myths not dealing with creation, the Shasta and the, Achomawi are more similar to one another. Both possess many Coyote stories, the major part of which they have in common. The Achomawi, however, share a number of episodes in such stories with the Maidu and not with the Shasta. On the other hand, Coyote in a number of these tales among the Shasta is less purely a trickster than among the Achomawi, as he figures several times as an important character, a benefactor of mankind, and a destroyer of monsters. (The same evidently holds true among the Shasta as among other tribes where Coyote alone takes the place of the contrasting personages of the creator and himself, as among the Pomo, Southern Wintun, and Miwok: while he does not lose his tricky nature, he assumes at least certain of the more dignified attributes of the creator or culture-hero.)

Among miscellaneous tales the Achomawi possess the story of the loon-woman, the theft of fire, the two girls sent in search of a husband, the struggle between the lizard and the grizzly-bear, and the lost brother. In the course of the latter the mice ascend to the sky to seek information from the sun regarding the lost brother. Among the Shasta a number of such stories appear. That of the lost brother assumes a different form, being apparently part of a series of tales relating to two culture-hero brothers, one of whom wanders about the country killing monsters. The surviving brother's quest is more elaborately described, and the ascent to the sky is also expanded. A number of incidents in this story recall the type of tales characteristic of the region of western Washington. Other incidents in this and other stories also suggest connection with the Puget Sound region. There are some Wintun resemblances. There is but little which directly resembles the mythology of the Northwestern area, although the Shasta are in immediate contact with it (p. 14)

[18] Contrib. to N. A. Ethn., II, 1890, part 1, especially pp. 94 seq., lxxix seq. (p. 14)

[19] Ibid., lxxviii: "Jeremiah Curtin . . . obtained over one hundred Modoc myths in 1883 and 1884, now forming part of the unpublished collection of the Bureau of Ethnology." (p. 14)

[20] Two bodies of myths from other tribes in the northern Coast Range have been published since the writing of this paper. Mr. S. A. Barrett has given "A Composite Myth of the Pomo Indians" of upper Clear lake, in the Journ. Am. Folk-lore, XIX, 37, 1906. Coyote, who is licentious, by trickery has two children, who are abused. In revenge Coyote sets fire to the world, escaping to the sky. He is sent back to earth by Madumda, his elder brother, the chief deity. Coyote eats the food he finds roasted, becomes thirsty, but cannot find drink until he reaches the ocean. He becomes sick, is doctored by Kuksu, a mythical and ceremonial character, and the water that flows from his belly forms Clear lake. What he has eaten turns to water animals. He builds houses, and from feathers placed in these makes people. Going to the owners of the sun, he causes them to sleep. The mice have gnawed the string by which the sun is hung, and Coyote brings it back to Clear lake. Various birds try, and the crow brothers succeed, in placing the

sun in the sky. Coyote then transforms the people he has made into animals, assigning each its attributes.

Dr. P. E. Goddard gives a number of "Lassik Tales" from the Athabascans of Van Duzen and Dobbin creeks on the east side of lower Eel river, Humboldt county, in the Journ. Am. Folk-lore, XIX, 133, 1906. The first is a version of the story of panther, wild-cat, and Coyote found also among {footnote p. 187} the Yuki and in a somewhat different form among the Shasta and Maidu. Wild-cat and fox are forced by Coyote to show him how their elder brother kills (leer in a magic enclosure. Coyote bungles and the deer escape. Panther returns and kills his two younger brothers, but they return to life. The second tale is of the bear and deer children. As in many versions, the deer children finally escape over the neck or leg of the crane, who drops the pursuing bear into the river. The third story tells of the theft of the sun by Coyote disguised as a woman, much as in the Yuki and Porno versions. The fourth story relates bow the wren made a pet or dog of the grizzly bear. In the fifth the enemy are destroyed and the scalps of the slain recovered with the help of Coyote's trickery and the gnawing of bow-strings by the mice. The sixth tells how a boy and his grandmother alone are not killed. The boy grows up, killing small animals. He is caught (presumably by tile slayer of his kindred), escapes, and the pursuer is killed by his grandmother while gambling. Dr. Goddard states that stories similar to these two are found among the Tolowa of Del Norte county. Parallels also occur to the fifth among the Shasta and Yana, to the sixth among the Maidu, the Yana, and the Yokuts. In the seventh story Thunder, gambling, wins from Coyote all his property, and then having told him the means of his winning, rises to the sky. According to the eighth, two brothers follow an elk until the elder becomes a tottering old man. He kills the elk that has impaled his brother, and turns to an otter. In the ninth, a tale rather than a myth, a dog returning from the hunt is asked how many deer have been killed. When he speaks, all who hear die (p. 19)

[21] Op. cit., Miwok, 358, 366, 368, Yokuts, 383, Shoshonean, 394, 395. (p. 19)

[22] Journ. Am. Folk-Lore, XV, 104-106, 1902. (p. 20)

[23] Published by the Country Club, 1904, p. 34. (p. 21)

[24] California Farmer, April 27, 1860 (p. 22)

[25]Partially based on a Rumsien text. (p. 32)

[26] Partially based on a Rumsien text. (p. 34)

[27] The Miwok of Yosemite also state that the thunders are two boys who were deer. They control snow and rain. (p. 42)

[28] C-oyo, nearly Shroyo; the t's in Kokwiteit are palatal, approaching ch. Kokwiteit resembles the word for raven in other dialects. (p. 56)

[29] The Yaudanchi have a myth about the Pleiades. They say that they were girls who rose to the sky. One was pregnant and could not rise. She turned to a rock. One or more stars near them are young men who followed them. (p. 59)

[30] From a Yaudanchi text. Present series, II, 263. (p. 72)

[31] From a Yaudanchi text. Present series, II, 259. (p. 73)

[32] From a Yaudanchi text. Present series, II, 264. (p. 75)

[33] From a Yaudanchi text. Present series, II, 266 (p. 79)

[34] From a Yaudanchi text. Present series, II, 272. (p. 83)

[35] There is an obvious contradiction in causing continuous night by the absence of the night as well as of the sun and moon. Similarly in a Yurok myth, darkness, which at first was lacking in the world, was stolen from the twelve sun-moon brothers, or, in another version, results when the sun first moves across the sky instead of standing still (p. 91).

www.ingramcontent.com/pod-product-compliance
Lightning Source LLC
Chambersburg PA
CBHW061105100726
47911CB00012B/409

* 9 7 8 1 3 9 6 3 2 5 7 4 8 *